Contents

P9-CDL-098

Introduction   **6**
William Shakespeare: life, plays, theater, verse   8
Macbeth: date, source, text   15

MACBETH
Original text and modern version   17

Activities   **206**
Characters   206
Themes and images   212
Close reading   216
Examination questions   220
One-word-answer quiz   222
What's missing?   223

Introduction

Shakespeare Made Easy is intended for readers approaching the plays for the first time, who find the language of Elizabethan poetic drama an initial obstacle to understanding and enjoyment. In the past, the only answer to the problem has been to grapple with the difficulties with the aid of explanatory footnotes (often missing when they are most needed) and a stern teacher. Generations of students have complained that "Shakespeare was ruined for me at school."

Usually a fuller appreciation of Shakespeare's plays comes in later life. Often the desire to read Shakespeare for pleasure and enrichment follows from a visit to the theater, where excellence of acting and production can bring to life qualities which sometimes lie dormant on the printed page.

Shakespeare Made Easy can never be a substitute for the original plays. It cannot possibly convey the full meaning of Shakespeare's poetic expression, which is untranslatable. *Shakespeare Made Easy* concentrates on the dramatic aspect, enabling the novice to become familiar with the plot and characters, and to experience one facet of Shakespeare's genius. To know and understand the central issues of each play is a sound starting point for further exploration and development.

Discretion can be used in choosing the best method to employ. One way is to read the original Shakespeare first, ignoring the modern version – or using it only when interest or understanding flags. Another way is to read the translation first, to establish confidence and familiarity with plot and characters.

Either way, cross-reference can be illuminating. The modern text can explain what is being said if Shakespeare's language is particularly complex or his expression antiquated. The Shakespeare text will show the reader of the modern paraphrase how much more can be expressed in poetry than in prose.

SHAKESPEARE MADE EASY

MODERN ENGLISH VERSION
SIDE-BY-SIDE WITH FULL ORIGINAL TEXT

Macbeth

EDITED AND RENDERED INTO MODERN ENGLISH BY
Alan Durband

BARRON'S

First U.S. edition published 1985 by Barron's Educational Series, Inc.

Hutchinson & Co. (Publishers) Ltd
An imprint of the Hutchinson Publishing Group
17-21 Conway Street, London W1P 6JD

Hutchinson Publishing Group (Australia) Pty Ltd
PO Box 496, 16-22 Church Street, Hawthorne,
Melbourne, Victoria 3122

Hutchinson Group (NZ) Ltd
32-34 View Road, PO Box 40-086, Glenfield, Aukland 10

Hutchinson Group (SA) (Pty) Ltd
PO Box 337, Bergvlei 2012, South Africa

First publishing 1984
© Alan Durband 1984

All inquiries should be addressed to:
Barron's Educational Series, Inc.
250 Wireless Boulevard
Hauppauge, NY 11788
http://www.barronseduc.com

ISBN-13: 978-0-8120-3571-1
ISBN-10: 0-8120-3571-2

Library of Congress Catalog No. 84-28351

Library of Congress Cataloging in Publication Data
Shakespeare, William, 1564–1616.
    Macbeth.

    (Shakespeare made easy)
    Summary: Presents the original text of Shakespeare's play side by side with a modern
version, discusses the author and the theater of his time, and provides quizzes and other
study activities.
    1. Shakespeare, William, 1564–1616. Macbeth.
2. Shakespeare, William, 1564–1616—Study and teaching.
[1. Shakespeare, William, 1564–1616. Macbeth. 2. Plays.
3. Shakespeare, William, 1564–1616—Study and teaching.]
I. Durband, Alan. II. Title. III. Series: Shakespeare, William,
1564–1616. Shakespeare made easy.
PR2823.A25D8   1985   822.3'3   84-28351
ISBN 0-8120-3571-2

PRINTED IN THE UNITED STATES OF AMERICA
58

'Reade him, therefore; and againe, and againe: And if then you do not like him, surely you are in some danger, not to understand him....'

John Hemming
Henry Condell

Preface to the 1623 Folio Edition

Shakespeare Made Easy
Titles in the series
As You Like It
Hamlet
Julius Caesar
King Lear
Macbeth
The Merchant of Venice
A Midsummer Night's Dream
Much Ado About Nothing
Othello
Romeo and Juliet
The Taming of the Shrew
The Tempest
Twelfth Night

The use of *Shakespeare Made Easy* means that the newcomer need never be overcome by textual difficulties. From first to last, a measure of understanding is at hand – the key is provided for what has been a locked door to many students in the past. And as understanding grows, so an awareness develops of the potential of language as a vehicle for philosophic and moral expression, beauty and the abidingly memorable.

Even professional Shakespearean scholars can never hope to arrive at a complete understanding of the plays. Each critic, researcher, actor or producer merely adds a little to the work that has already been done, or makes fresh interpretations of the texts for new generations. For everyone, Shakespearean appreciation is a journey. *Shakespeare Made Easy* is intended to help with the first steps.

William Shakespeare

His life

William Shakespeare was born in Stratford-on-Avon, Warwickshire, on April 23, 1564, the son of a prosperous wool and leather merchant. Very little is known of his early life. From parish records we know that he married Ann Hathaway in 1582, when he was eighteen, and she was twenty-six. They had three children, the eldest of whom died in childhood.

Between his marriage and the next thing we know about him, there is a gap of ten years. Probably he became a member of a traveling company of actors. By 1592 he had settled in London and had earned a reputation as an actor and playwright.

Theaters were then in their infancy. The first (called *The Theatre*) was built in 1576. Two more followed as the taste for theater grew: *The Curtain* in 1577 and *The Rose* in 1587. The demand for new plays naturally increased. Shakespeare probably earned a living adapting old plays and working in collaboration with others on new ones. Today we would call him a "freelance," since he was not permanently attached to one theater.

In 1594, a new company of actors, The Lord Chamberlain's Men, was formed, and Shakespeare was one of the shareholders. He remained a member throughout his working life. The company regrouped in 1603 and was renamed The King's Men, with James I as its patron.

Shakespeare and his fellow-actors prospered. In 1598 they built their own theater, *The Globe*, which broke away from the traditional rectangular shape of the inn and its yard (the early home of traveling bands of actors). Shakespeare described it in *Henry V* as "this wooden O," because it was circular.

Many other theaters were built by investors eager to profit from the new enthusiasm for drama. *The Hope*, *The Fortune*,

The Red Bull and *The Swan* were all open-air "public" theaters. There were also many "private" (or indoor) theaters, one of which (*The Blackfriars*) was purchased by Shakespeare and his friends because the child actors who performed there were dangerous competitors. (Shakespeare denounces them in *Hamlet.*)

After writing some thirty-seven plays (the exact number is something which scholars argue about), Shakespeare retired to his native Stratford, wealthy and respected. He died on his birthday, in 1616.

His plays

Shakespeare's plays were not all published in his lifetime. None of them comes to us exactly as he wrote it.

In Elizabethan times, plays were not regarded as either literature or good reading matter. They were written at speed (often by more than one writer), performed perhaps ten or twelve times, and then discarded. Fourteen of Shakespeare's plays were first printed in Quarto (17cm × 21cm) volumes, not all with his name as the author. Some were authorized (the "good" Quartos) and probably were printed from prompt copies provided by the theater. Others were pirated (the "bad" Quartos) by booksellers who may have employed shorthand writers, or bought actors' copies after the run of the play had ended.

In 1623, seven years after Shakespeare's death, John Hemming and Henry Condell (fellow-actors and shareholders in The King's Men) published a collected edition of Shakespeare's works – thirty-six plays in all – in a Folio (21cm × 34cm) edition. From their introduction it would seem that they used Shakespeare's original manuscripts ("we have scarce received from him a blot in his papers") but the Folio volumes that still survive are not all exactly alike, nor are the plays printed as we know them today, with act and scene divisions and stage directions.

A modern edition of a Shakespeare play is the result of a great deal of scholarly research and editorial skill over several centuries. The aim is always to publish a text (based on the good and bad Quartos and the Folio editions) that most closely resembles what Shakespeare intended. Misprints have added to the problems, so some words and lines are pure guesswork. This explains why some versions of Shakespeare's plays differ from others.

His theater

The first playhouse built as such in Elizabethan London, constructed in 1576, was *The Theatre*. Its co-founders were John Brayne, an investor, and James Burbage, a carpenter turned actor. Like the six or seven "public" (or outdoor) theaters which followed it over the next thirty years, it was situated outside the city, to avoid conflict with the authorities. They disapproved of players and playgoing, partly on moral and political grounds, and partly because of the danger of spreading the plague. (There were two major epidemics during Shakespeare's lifetime, and on each occasion the theaters were closed for lengthy periods.)

The Theatre was a financial success, and Shakespeare's company performed there until 1598, when a dispute over the lease of the land forced Burbage to take down the building. It was re-created in Southwark, as *The Globe*, with Shakespeare and several of his fellow-actors as the principal shareholders.

By modern standards, *The Globe* was small. Externally, the octagonal building measured less than thirty meters across, but in spite of this it could accommodate an audience of between two and three thousand people. (The largest of the three theaters at the National Theatre complex in London today seats 1160.)

Performances were advertised by means of playbills posted around the city, and they took place during the hours of daylight when the weather was suitable. A flag flew to show that all was well, to save playgoers a wasted journey.

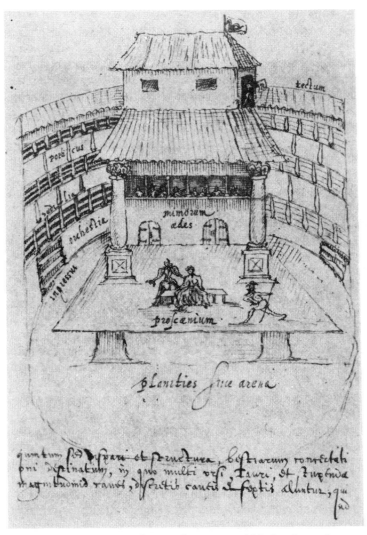

Interior of the Swan Theatre – from a pen and ink drawing made in 1596 (Mansell Collection)

At the entrance, a doorkeeper collected one penny (about 60 cents today) for admission to the "pit" – a name taken from the old inn-yards, where bear-baiting and cock-fighting were popular sports. This was the minimum charge for seeing a play. The "groundlings," as they were called, simply stood around the three sides of the stage, in the open air. Those who were better off could pay extra for a seat under cover. Stairs led from the pit to three tiers of galleries around the walls. The higher one went, the more one paid. The best seats cost one shilling (or $7 today). In theaters owned by speculators like Francis Langley and Philip Henslowe, half the gallery takings went to the landlord.

A full house might consist of 800 groundlings and 1500 in the galleries, with a dozen more exclusive seats on the stage itself for the gentry. A new play might run for between six and sixteen performances; the average was about ten. As there were no breaks between scenes, and no intervals, most plays could be performed in two hours. A trumpet sounded three times before the play began.

The acting company assembled in the Tiring House at the rear of the stage. This was where they attired (or dressed) themselves: not in costumes representing the period of the play, but in Elizabethan doublet and hose. All performances were therefore in modern dress, though no expense was spared to make the stage costumes lavish. The entire company was male. By law actresses were not allowed, and female roles were performed by boys.

Access to the stage from the Tiring House was through two doors, one on each side of the stage. Because there was no front curtain, every entrance had to have its corresponding exit, so an actor killed on stage had to be carried off. There was no scenery: the audience used its imagination, guided by the spoken word. Storms and night scenes might well be performed on sunny days in mid-afternoon; the Elizabethan playgoer relied entirely on the playwright's descriptive skills to establish the dramatic atmosphere.

Once on stage, the actors and their expensive clothes were protected from sudden showers by a canopy, the underside of which was painted blue and spangled with stars to represent the heavens. A trapdoor in the stage made ghostly entrances and the gravedigging scene in *Hamlet* possible. Behind the main stage, in between the two entrance doors, there was a curtained area, concealing a small inner stage, useful for bedroom scenes. Above this was a balcony, which served for castle walls (as in *Henry V*) or a domestic balcony (as in the famous scene in *Romeo and Juliet*).

The acting style in Elizabethan times was probably more declamatory than we favor today, but the close proximity of the audience also made a degree of intimacy possible. In those days soliloquies and asides seemed quite natural. Act and scene divisions did not exist (those in printed versions of the play today have been added by editors), but Shakespeare often indicates a scene-ending by a rhyming couplet.

A company such as The King's Men at *The Globe* would consist of around twenty-five actors, half of whom might be shareholders, and the rest part-timers engaged for a particular play. Among the shareholders in *The Globe* were several specialists – William Kempe, for example, was a renowned comedian and Robert Armin was a singer and dancer. Playwrights wrote parts to suit the actors who were available, and devised ways of overcoming the absence of women. Shakespeare often has his heroines dress as young men, and physical contact between lovers was formal compared with the realism we expect today.

His verse

Shakespeare wrote his plays mostly in blank verse: that is, unrhymed lines consisting of ten syllables, alternately stressed and unstressed. The technical term for this form is the iambic pentameter. When Shakespeare first began to write for the

13

stage, it was fashionable to maintain this regular beat from the first line of the play till the last.

Shakespeare conformed at first and then experimented. Some of his early plays contain whole scenes in rhyming couplets – in *Romeo and Juliet*, for example, there is extensive use of rhyme, and as if to show his versatility, Shakespeare even inserts a sonnet into the dialog.

But as he matured, he sought greater freedom of expression than rhyme allowed. Rhyme is still used to indicate a scene ending, or to stress lines which he wishes the audience to remember. Generally, though, Shakespeare moved toward the rhythms of everyday speech. This gave him many dramatic advantages, which he fully and subtly exploits in terms of atmosphere, character, emotion, stress and pace.

It is Shakespeare's poetic imagery, however, that most distinguishes his verse from that of lesser playwrights. It enables him to stretch the imagination, express complex thought-patterns in memorable language and convey a number of associated ideas in a compressed and economical form. A study of Shakespeare's imagery – especially in his later plays – is often the key to a full understanding of his meaning and purposes.

At the other extreme is prose. Shakespeare normally reserves it for servants, clowns, commoners and pedestrian matters such as lists, messages and letters.

Macbeth

Date

Though not published until the Folio Edition in 1623, Shakespeare wrote the play in 1606, probably for a performance before the King of Denmark, who was in London on a visit to his brother-in-law, James I. Being The King's Men, the company wished to please their patron, and Shakespeare's choice of the Macbeth story gave them that opportunity. History was distorted somewhat in the process.

Source

The real Macbeth reigned between 1040 and 1057. His immediate predecessors were Malcolm II (1005–34) and Duncan I (1034–40). Macbeth killed Duncan, and Duncan's son Malcolm eventually revenged his father's murder in 1057, reigning as Malcolm III. He died a natural death in 1093.

Shakespeare found the nucleus of the play in a book which he used many times in writing his History plays: Ralph Holinshed's *Chronicles of England, Scotland and Ireland* (first published in 1577 and reissued in 1587). According to Holinshed, Duncan I was a weak king, and Macbeth a rival chief with a genuine grievance. This Macbeth had met "three women in evil apparel," who made certain prophecies. Encouraged by his wife, and aided by a certain Banquo and some of his friends, he killed Duncan and reigned honorably for many years.

Eventually, he feared for his safety and embarked on a series of murders. Banquo was his first victim, but Banquo's son Fleance escaped, to found the House of Stuart. This meant he was, of course, the ancestor of James VI of Scotland, who became James I of England.

Also in Holinshed's *Chronicles* there is a story of an old warrior chieftain called King Duff, who was murdered by a man called Donwald and his wife, when the king was staying in their castle as a guest. Shakespeare combined the two stories in composing the plot of *Macbeth*. Adaptations and alterations of this kind were common in Shakespeare's day.

Shakespeare also condenses Macbeth's reign into a short period of about ten weeks. He compresses (for dramatic purposes) the various rebellions and invasions – the rebel MacDonald, King Sweno of Norway, and the traitorous Thane of Cawdor appear to be attacking at much the same time.

Text

The play as we know it seems to have been revised and altered in the seventeen years between its first performance and publication. Some speeches and several scenes (for example, those involving Hecate and the Witches) bear strong evidence of the hand of Thomas Middleton, whose own play *The Witch* was published in 1612. The shortness of the play also suggests abridgment. What we know today as *Macbeth* is almost certainly not exactly what Shakespeare wrote.

Macbeth

Original text and modern version

The characters

Duncan   King of Scotland
Malcolm ⎫
Donalbain ⎬ his sons
Macbeth   a general in the king's army, later king
Banquo   a general
Macduff
Lennox ⎫
Ross ⎪
Mentieth ⎬ noblemen of Scotland
Angus ⎪
Caithness ⎭
Fleance   Banquo's son
Siward   Earl of Northumberland
Young Siward   his son
Seton   personal officer to Macbeth
Macduff's Son
An English Doctor
A Scottish Doctor
A Sergeant
A Porter
An Old Man
Three Murderers
Lady Macbeth
Lady Macduff
A Lady-in-waiting
Three Witches
Hecate
Apparitions
Lords, Gentlemen, Officers, Soldiers, Attendants and Messengers

Act one

Scene 1

A desert place. Thunder and lightning. Enter three **Witches**.

1st Witch   When shall we three meet again
  In thunder, lightning, or in rain?

2nd Witch   When the hurlyburly's done,
  When the battle's lost and won.

5 **3rd Witch**   That will be ere the set of sun.

1st Witch   Where the place?

2nd Witch   Upon the heath.

3rd Witch   There to meet with Macbeth.

1st Witch   I come, Graymalkin!

10 **2nd Witch**   Paddock calls.

3rd Witch   Anon!

All   Fair is foul, and foul is fair:
  Hover through the fog and filthy air.

[They vanish]

Act one

Scene 1

A deserted heath in Scotland on a stormy night. The year is 1040, during the reign of King Duncan. Three **Witches** *chant around a steaming cauldron.*

1st Witch   When shall we three meet again
In thunder, lightning and in rain?

2nd Witch   When the ruckus is all done.
When the battle's lost and won.

3rd Witch   Before the setting of the sun.

1st Witch   Where's the place?

2nd Witch   Upon the heath.

3rd Witch   There to meet Macbeth.

1st Witch   [*as if commanded*] I'm coming, Cat!

2nd Witch   The toad calls!

3rd Witch   Coming!

Together   Fair is foul, and foul is fair.
We hover through the fog and filthy air.

[*They disappear*]

Scene 2

A camp near Forres. Alarum. Enter **King Duncan, Malcolm, Donalbain, Lennox**, *with attendants, meeting a bleeding* **Sergeant**.

Duncan   What bloody man is that? He can report,
As seemeth by his plight, of the revolt
The newest state.

Malcolm   This is the sergeant,
Who like a good and hardy soldier fought
5   'Gainst my captivity . . . Hail, brave friend!
Say to the king the knowledge of the broil
As thou didst leave it.

Sergeant   Doubtful it stood;
As two spent swimmers that do cling together
And choke their art . . . The merciless Macdonwald –
10   Worthy to be a rebel, for to that
The multiplying villainies of nature
Do swarm upon him – from the Western Isles
Of kerns and gallowglasses is supplied;
And Fortune, on his damned quarrel smiling,
15   Showed like a rebel's whore: but all's too weak:
For brave Macbeth – well he deserves that name –
Disdaining fortune, with his brandished steel,
Which smoked with bloody execution,
Like Valour's minion carved out his passage
20   Till he faced the slave;
Which ne'er shook hands, nor bade farewell to him,
Till he unseamed him from the nave to the chops,
And fixed his head upon our battlements.

Duncan   O, valiant cousin! worthy gentleman!

Scene 2

A military camp near the town of Forres in Scotland. A battle is raging nearby. Rebels are fighting the king's troops. A trumpet sounds. Duncan (King of Scotland) enters, with Malcolm and Donalbain (his sons) and several Lords and Attendants. They meet a Sergeant, whose uniform is stained with blood.

Duncan   Who's that man, bleeding so badly? Judging by his wounds, he can give us the latest news of the rebellion.

Malcolm   It's the sergeant! He saved me from capture. [*Helping the* **Sergeant** *to stand*] Tell the king how the battle was going when you left it.

Sergeant   It was in the balance. Like two tired swimmers, the armies clung together, dragging each other down. Then that cruel, villainous, arch-rebel Macdonwald got some reinforcements – Irish mercenaries from the Hebrides. Lady Luck, the whore, favored him at first. But it wasn't enough. Brave Macbeth – he well deserves that name! – just ignored the odds. With sword steaming with blood, he carved his way forward till he faced the wretch. There were no fancy formalities. He ripped the traitor apart from his guts to his gullet and stuck his head upon our battlements!

Duncan   Well done, brave cousin!

25 **Sergeant**   As whence the sun 'gins his reflection
Shipwracking storms and direful thunders break;
So from that spring whence comfort seemed to come
Discomfort swells. Mark, king of Scotland, mark!
No sooner justice had, with valour armed,
30 Compelled these skipping kerns to trust their heels,
But the Norweyan lord, surveying vantage,
With furbished arms and new supplies of men,
Began a fresh assault.

Duncan   Dismayed not this
Our captains, Macbeth and Banquo?

Sergeant   Yes;
35 As sparrows, eagles; or the hare, the lion:
If I say sooth, I must report they were
As cannons overcharged with double cracks,
So they doubly redoubled strokes upon the foe:
Except they meant to bathe in reeking wounds,
40 Or memorize another Golgotha,
I cannot tell:
But I am faint, my gashes cry for help.

Duncan   So well thy words become thee, as thy wounds;
They smack of honour both. Go get him surgeons.

[*Exit* **Sergeant**, *attended*]

45 Who comes here?

[*Enter* **Ross** *and* **Angus**]

Malcolm   The worthy thane of Ross.

Lennox   What a haste looks through his eyes! So should he
look
That seems to speak things strange.

Sergeant   After sunshine there can be a storm. Following good news, there is often bad. Listen, King of Scotland, listen! Our valiant men, fighting their just cause, had no sooner forced these troops to show how fast they could retreat than the king of Norway saw his chance. He launched a fresh attack with new supplies and reinforcements.

Duncan   Macbeth and Banquo – did they lose heart?

Sergeant   Do sparrows scare eagles or lions fear hares? They were like cannons with a double load of shot. They fought twice as hard! As if they wished to swim in blood or copy Calvary. [*He staggers*] I'm feeling faint. My wounds need treatment . . .

Duncan   You can be proud of them, Sergeant. They do you honor, like your report. [*To an* **Attendant**] Get him to a doctor.

[*The* **Sergeant** *and* **Attendant** *leave.* **Ross** *and* **Angus,** *two loyal nobles, arrive in haste*]

Who's this?

Malcolm   The worthy thane of Ross.

Lennox   He looks as though he has some startling news.

Ross   God save the king!

Duncan   Whence cam'st thou, worthy thane?

Ross   From Fife, great king,
Where the Norweyan banners flout the sky,
50   And fan our people cold.
Norway himself, with terrible numbers,
Assisted by that most disloyal traitor
The thane of Cawdor, began a dismal conflict,
Till that Bellona's bridegroom, lapped in proof,
55   Confronted him with self-comparisons,
Point against point, rebellious arm 'gainst arm,
Curbing his lavish spirit: and, to conclude,
The victory fell on us.

Duncan   Great happiness!

Ross   That now
60   Sweno, the Norways' king, craves composition;
Nor would we deign him burial of his men
Till he disbursed, at Saint Colme's Inch,
Ten thousand dollars to our general use.

Duncan   No more that thane of Cawdor shall deceive
65   Our bosom interest: go pronounce his present death,
And with his former title greet Macbeth.

Ross   I'll see it done.

Duncan   What he hath lost, noble Macbeth hath won.

                                   [*Exeunt*]

Ross   God save the king!

Duncan   Where have you come from, good thane?

Ross   From Fife, great King, where the Norwegians terrorize our people. Backed by that traitor, Cawdor, the king of Norway launched a massive attack. But he met his match in Macbeth. Wedded to war and armored for it, Macbeth fought hand to hand, sword against sword, till he'd brought him to his knees. In short, we won!

Duncan   Splendid!

Ross   Now, King Sweno of Norway is suing for peace. We wouldn't let him bury his dead till he'd paid ten thousand pounds at Inchcolme.

Duncan   That thane of Cawdor won't deceive us twice. [*To* **Attendants**] Go – see he's executed immediately. [*To* **Ross**] Cawdor's title shall pass to Macbeth. Greet him with it.

Ross   I'll see it's done.

Duncan   Cawdor's loss is noble Macbeth's gain!

[*They go*]

Scene 3

A heath. Thunder. Enter the three **Witches**.

1st Witch   Where hast thou been, sister?

2nd Witch   Killing swine.

3rd Witch   Sister, where thou?

1st Witch   A sailor's wife had chestnuts in her lap,
And munched, and munched, and munched: 'Give me',
5   quoth I.
'Aroint thee, witch!' the rump-fed ronyon cries.
Her husband's to Aleppo gone, master o'th' Tiger:
But in a sieve I'll thither sail,
And, like a rat without a tail,
10   I'll do, I'll do, and I'll do.

2nd Witch   I'll give thee a wind.

1st Witch   Th'art kind.

3rd Witch   And I another.

1st Witch   I myself have all the other,
15   And the very ports they blow,
All the quarters that they know
I'th' shipman's card.
I will drain him dry as hay:
Sleep shall neither night nor day
20   Hang upon his pent-house lid;
He shall live a man forbid:
Weary se'nights nine times nine
Shall he dwindle, peak, and pine:
Though his bark cannot be lost,
25   Yet it shall be tempest-tost.
Look what I have.

Scene 3

The heath again, in a thunderstorm. The three **Witches** *meet.*

1st Witch   Where have you been, sister?

2nd Witch   Killing swine!

3rd Witch   Sister, where have you?

1st Witch   Listen. A sailor's wife had chestnuts in her lap.
She munched and munched and munched.
"Give me one," I said.
"Begone, you witch," the bloated baggage cried.
Her husband's gone to sea aboard the *Tiger* —
But in a sieve I'll follow him
And like a rat without a tail,
I'll do for him, do for him, I'll do for him!

2nd Witch   I'll give you a wind.

1st Witch   You're kind.

3rd Witch   I'll give you another.

1st Witch   I'm in charge of all the others.
I control the ports they blow from —
Every compass point we know from
Records, maps and charts.
I will see he's nothing to drink —
Ensure he never sleeps a wink!
Cursed he'll be, and live confined!
For weary weeks, yes, nine times nine,
He shall dwindle, peak and pine!
Though his ship cannot be lost,
Yet it shall be tempest-tossed.
Look what I have.

2nd Witch   Show me, show me.

1st Witch   Here I have a pilot's thumb,
Wrecked as homeward he did come.

[*Drum within*]

30 **3rd Witch**   A drum, a drum!
Macbeth doth come.

All   The Weird Sisters, hand in hand,
Posters of the sea and land,
Thus do go, about, about,
35   Thrice to thine, and thrice to mine,
And thrice again, to make up nine.
Peace! the charm's wound up.

[*Enter* **Macbeth** *and* **Banquo**]

Macbeth   So foul and fair a day I have not seen.

Banquo   How far is't called to Forres? What are these,
40   So withered, and so wild in their attire,
That look not like th'inhabitants o'th'earth,
And yet are on't? Live you? or are you aught
That man may question? You seem to understand me,
By each at once her choppy finger laying
45   Upon her skinny lips: you should be women,
And yet your beards forbid me to interpret
That you are so.

Macbeth   Speak, if you can: what are you?

1st Witch   All hail, Macbeth! hail to thee, thane of Glamis!

2nd Witch   All hail, Macbeth! hail to thee, thane of Cawdor!

50 **3rd Witch**   All hail, Macbeth! that shalt be king hereafter.

2nd Witch   Show me, show me.

1st Witch   Here I have a pilot's thumb
Wrecked as he did homeward come.

[*A drum sounds*]

3rd Witch   A drum, a drum,
Macbeth does come!

[*They circle the cauldron, first one way, then the other,
chanting*]

Together   The Weird Sisters, hand in hand,
Travelers of the sea and land,
Thus go roundabout, about,
Three times your way, three times mine,
Three more again to make up nine.
Stop! The charm's prepared!

[**Macbeth** *enters, returning from the battlefield where he has
fought with honor. He is accompanied by* **Banquo**, *a fellow
nobleman*]

Macbeth   I've never seen a day so foul and fair.

Banquo   How far are we from Forres? [*He sees the* **Witches**]
What are these creatures so wrinkled and so wildly dressed?
They don't look human. [*To the* **Witches**] Are you living
beings? Or spirits we can question? [*The* **Witches** *put their
fingers to their lips*] You seem to understand me from the way
you put your crooked fingers on your skinny lips. [*He stares at
their hairy chins*] You look like women, but you have beards.

Macbeth   Speak – if you can. Who are you?

1st Witch   All hail, Macbeth! Hail to you, Thane of Glamis!

2nd Witch   All hail, Macbeth! Hail to you, Thane of Cawdor!

3rd Witch   All hail, Macbeth! You'll be king one day!

Banquo   Good sir, why do you start, and seem to fear
Things that do sound so fair? I'th' name of truth,
Are ye fantastical, or that indeed
Which outwardly ye show? My noble partner
55 You greet with present grace and great prediction
Of noble having and of royal hope,
That he seems rapt withall: to me you speak not.
If you can look into the seeds of time,
And say which grain will grow and which will not,
60 Speak then to me, who neither beg nor fear
Your favours nor your hate.

1st Witch   Hail!

2nd Witch   Hail!

3rd Witch   Hail!

65 **1st Witch**   Lesser than Macbeth, and greater.

2nd Witch   Not so happy, yet much happier.

3rd Witch   Thou shalt get kings, though thou be none:
So all hail, Macbeth and Banquo!

1st Witch   Banquo and Macbeth, all hail!

70 **Macbeth**   Stay, you imperfect speakers, tell me more:
By Sinel's death I know I am thane of Glamis;
But how of Cawdor? the thane of Cawdor lives
A prosperous gentleman; and to be king
Stands not within the prospect of belief,
75 No more than to be Cawdor. Say from whence
You owe this strange intelligence, or why
Upon this blasted heath you stop our way
With such prophetic greeting? Speak, I charge you.

[They vanish]

Banquo   [*To* **Macbeth**] Why be so startled? Why fear what sounds so fine?
[*To the* **Witches**] The truth now! Are you supernatural? Or are you as mortal as you look? You greeted my noble companion by his present title. Then you prophesied new honors, with hopes of royalty. Now he's lost in thought. To me you say nothing. If you really can foretell the future – if you know who'll prosper and who won't – speak to me! I don't seek your favors and I don't fear your hate!

1st Witch   Hail!

2nd Witch   Hail!

3rd Witch   Hail!

1st Witch   Lesser than Macbeth, and greater . . .

2nd Witch   Not so happy, yet much happier . . .

3rd Witch   You shall father kings, yet not be one yourself. So all hail, Macbeth and Banquo!

1st Witch   Banquo and Macbeth, all hail!

[*They turn to go*]

Macbeth   [*Coming to himself*] Stop. You've only told me half the story. Tell me more. I know I'm thane of Glamis, since Sinel, my father, died. But how can I be thane of Cawdor? Cawdor is alive, a prosperous gentleman. As for being king, that's beyond belief – as impossible as being thane of Cawdor. Where did you get this story from? And why stop us on this godforsaken heath to tell us of these prophecies? Answer me!

[*The* **Witches** *vanish*]

Banquo   The earth hath bubbles, as the water has,
80   And these are of them: whither are they vanished?

Macbeth   Into the air; and what seemed corporal, melted,
As breath into the wind. Would they had stayed!

Banquo   Were such things here as we do speak about?
Or have we eaten on the insane root
85   That takes the reason prisoner?

Macbeth   Your children shall be kings.

Banquo   You shall be king.

Macbeth   And thane of Cawdor too: went it not so?

Banquo   To th'selfsame tune and words. Who's here?

[*Enter* **Ross** *and* **Angus**]

Ross   The king hath happily received, Macbeth,
90   The news of thy success: and when he reads
Thy personal venture in the rebels' fight,
His wonders and his praises do contend
Which should be thine or his: silenced with that,
In viewing o'er the rest o'th' self-same day,
95   He finds thee in the stout Norweyan ranks,
Nothing afeard of what thyself didst make
Strange images of death. As thick as hail
Came post with post, and every one did bear
Thy praises in his kingdom's great defence,
And poured them down before him.

100 **Angus**   We are sent
To give thee from our royal master thanks,
Only to herald thee into his sight,
Not pay thee.

Ross   And for an earnest of a greater honour,

Banquo   Water can turn into bubbles and evaporate, so the earth can too. Where have they gone?

Macbeth   Into the air. What seemed solid has melted away like breath into the wind. I wish they had stayed!

Banquo   Were they really here, or have we gone mad?

Macbeth   [*Brooding*] Your children shall be kings.

Banquo   You shall be king.

Macbeth   And thane of Cawdor too. That's what they said?

Banquo   Exactly. Who's here?

[**Ross** *and* **Angus** *enter on their mission from* **King Duncan**]

Ross   The king was pleased to hear of your success, Macbeth. When he read of your valor against the rebels, wonder silenced him. He was speechless with admiration. Later that same day he finds you foremost among the Norwegians! Death—and you did some killing!—held no fears for you. Thick as hail, reports poured in, praising your part in the defense of Duncan's kingdom.

Angus   We come as escorts, with the king's thanks. Not with rewards . . .

Ross   . . . But as a sample of the honor yet to come, he

105   He bade me, from him, call thee thane of Cawdor:
      In which addition, hail, most worthy thane,
      For it is thine.

Banquo   [*Aside*]   What, can the devil speak true?

Macbeth   The thane of Cawdor lives: why do you dress me
      In borrowed robes?

Angus   Who was the thane lives yet,
110   But under heavy judgement bears that life
      Which he deserves to lose. Whether he was combined
      With those of Norway, or did line the rebel
      With hidden help and vantage, or that with both
      He laboured in his country's wreck, I know not;
115   But treasons capital, confessed, and proved,
      Have overthrown him.

Macbeth   [*Aside*]   Glamis, and thane of Cawdor:
      The greatest is behind. Thanks for your pains –
      [*To* **Banquo**] Do you not hope your children shall be kings,
      When those that gave the thane of Cawdor to me
      Promised no less to them?

120   **Banquo**   [*To* **Macbeth**]   That, trusted home,
      Might yet enkindle you unto the crown,
      Besides the thane of Cawdor. But 'tis strange:
      And oftentimes, to win us to our harm,
      The instruments of darkness tell us truths,
125   Win us with honest trifles, to betray's
      In deepest consequence.
      Cousins, a word, I pray you.

Macbeth   [*Aside*]   Two truths are told,
      As happy prologues to the swelling act
      Of the imperial theme. I thank you, gentlemen.
130   This supernatural soliciting
      Cannot be ill; cannot be good. If ill,

instructed me on his behalf to call you Thane of Cawdor. So, in that name, hail, most worthy thane! It's yours!

Banquo   [*To himself*] What? Can the devil speak true?

Macbeth   But the thane of Cawdor isn't dead. Why do you call me by his name?

Angus   The man who *was* the thane is still alive, but under sentence of death, which he deserves. Whether he allied himself with the Norwegians, or secretly aided the rebels, or did both, I don't know. But high treason has been proved and he's confessed.

Macbeth   [*To himself*] Thane of Glamis and thane of Cawdor! The greatest is yet to come. [*To* **Ross** *and* **Angus**] Thanks for all your trouble. [*To* **Banquo**] Don't you hope your children will be kings? Those who gave me the thaneship of Cawdor promised no less to them . . .

Banquo   Take that further, and you might be king, as well as thane of Cawdor. Strange. But sometimes to tempt us to evil, the devil wins our confidence with trifling bits of truth. Then he betrays us in the big things that really matter. [*To* **Ross** *and* **Angus**] Friends, a word with you if I may.

Macbeth   [*To himself*] Two predictions have come true. The first steps toward that ultimate goal, the throne! [*To* **Banquo, Ross** *and* **Angus**] Thanks, gentlemen. [*To himself again*] This meddling with the supernatural can be either evil or good. If

Why hath it given me earnest of success,
Commencing in a truth? I am Thane of Cawdor.
If good, why do I yield to that suggestion
135   Whose horrid image doth unfix my hair,
And make my seated heart knock at my ribs,
Against the use of nature? Present fears
Are less than horrible imaginings:
My thought, whose murder yet is but fantastical,
140   Shakes so my single state of man that function
Is smothered in surmise, and nothing is
But what is not.

Banquo   Look how our partner's rapt.

Macbeth   [*Aside*] If chance will have me king, why,
    chance may crown me,
Without my stir.

Banquo   New honours come upon him,
145   Like our strange garments, cleave not to their mould
But with the aid of use.

Macbeth   Come what come may,
Time and the hour runs through the roughest day.

Banquo   Worthy Macbeth, we stay upon your leisure.

Macbeth   Give me your favour: my dull brain was wrought
150   With things forgotten. Kind gentlemen, your pains
Are registered where every day I turn
The leaf to read them . . . Let us toward the king.
Think upon what hath chanced: and at more time,
The interim having weighed it, let us speak
Our free hearts each to other.

155 **Banquo**   Very gladly.

Macbeth   Till then, enough. Come, friends.

                                        [*Exeunt*]

it's evil, why has it given me a foretaste of success, beginning with something that's true? I *am* thane of Cawdor. If it's good, why am I thinking ghastly thoughts that make my hair stand on end and my heart thump unnaturally? Imagined horrors are worse than real fears. Just thinking about murder is enough to rattle my nerves and paralyze me. Only what's going on in my head seems real.

Banquo   [*To* **Ross** *and* **Angus**] Look how carried away our partner is.

Macbeth   [*Still to himself*] If fate says I'll be king, well, fate may crown me, without my help.

Banquo   [*To* **Ross** *and* **Angus**] New honors are like new clothes. It takes time to get used to them.

Macbeth   [*Still to himself*] Whatever happens, even the roughest day comes to an end.

Banquo   Worthy Macbeth! We are ready when you are.

Macbeth   [*Recovering*] Forgive me. My thoughts were elsewhere. Gentlemen, thank you, as always, for your kindness. Let us go to meet the king. [*To* **Banquo**] Think about what has happened, and after we've had time to weigh things, let's speak openly to each other.

Banquo   [*To* **Macbeth**] Gladly.

Macbeth   [*To* **Banquo**] Enough, for now. [*To* **Ross** *and* **Angus**] Come, friends.

[*They go*]

Scene 4

Forres. The Palace. Flourish. Enter **King Duncan, Malcolm, Donalbain, Lennox** *and* **Attendants**.

Duncan   Is execution done on Cawdor? Are not
Those in commission yet returned?

Malcolm   My liege,
They are not yet come back. But I have spoke
With one that saw him die: who did report
5   That very frankly he confessed his treasons,
Implored your highness' pardon, and set forth
A deep repentance: nothing in his life
Became him like the leaving it; he died
As one that had been studied in his death,
10   To throw away the dearest thing he owed
As 'twere a careless trifle.

Duncan   There's no art
To find the mind's construction in the face:
He was a gentleman on whom I built
An absolute trust.

[*Enter* **Macbeth, Banquo, Ross,** *and* **Angus**]

                            O worthiest cousin!
15   The sin of my ingratitude even now
Was heavy on me. Thou art so far before,
That swiftest wing of recompense is slow
To overtake thee. Would thou hadst less deserved,
That the proportion both of thanks and payment
20   Might have been mine! only I have left to say,
More is thy due than more than all can pay.

Scene 4

The palace at Forres. A fanfare. **King Duncan, Malcolm, Donalbain, Lennox** *and* **Attendants** *enter.*

Duncan   Has Cawdor been executed? Have the officers in charge returned?

Malcolm   Your Majesty, they have not yet come back. But I've spoken to someone who saw Cawdor die. He said he confessed his treasons very frankly, implored Your Highness's pardon and showed sincere repentance. He died far more honorably than he lived and seemed resolved to throw away his dearest possession – his life – as if it had no value.

Duncan   You can never tell from a man's face what's going on in his mind. I trusted him completely.

[**Macbeth, Banquo, Ross** *and* **Angus** *enter*]

Oh, worthiest cousin! I feel guilty of ingratitude. You have achieved so much so quickly that I cannot keep up with the debt I owe to you. I wish you had deserved less; then my thanks and rewards might have got ahead. I can only say that more is due to you than I can ever repay.

Macbeth   The service and the loyalty I owe,
In doing it, pays itself. Your highness' part
Is to receive our duties: and our duties
25 Are to your throne and state, children and servants;
Which do but what they should, by doing every thing
Safe toward your love and honour.

Duncan   Welcome hither:
I have begun to plant thee, and will labour
To make thee full of growing. Noble Banquo,
30 That hast no less deserved, nor must be known
No less to have done so: let me infold thee,
And hold thee to my heart.

Banquo   There if I grow,
The harvest is your own.

Duncan   My plenteous joys,
Wanton in fulness, seek to hide themselves
35 In drops of sorrow . . . Sons, kinsmen, thanes,
And you whose places are the nearest, know,
We will establish our estate upon
Our eldest, Malcolm, whom we name hereafter
The Prince of Cumberland: which honour must
40 Not unaccompanied invest him only,
But signs of nobleness, like stars, shall shine
On all deservers. From hence to Inverness,
And bind us further to you.

Macbeth   The rest is labour, which is not used for you:
45 I'll be myself the harbinger, and make joyful
The hearing of my wife with your approach;
So humbly take my leave.

Duncan   My worthy Cawdor!

Macbeth   The Prince of Cumberland! that is a step
On which I must fall down, or else o'er-leap,

Macbeth   [*Bowing*] Service to you as a loyal subject is its own reward. Your Highness must accept that service, which is to your throne and state, children and servants. We are only doing our duty when we protect your love and honor.

Duncan   Welcome here. I have begun to favor you and will see you prosper. And noble Banquo, you are no less deserving. Your worth must be recognized. Let me embrace you and hold you to my heart.

Banquo   If I prosper there, the benefits will all be yours.

Duncan   Joy overwhelms me to the point of tears. Sons, kinsmen, thanes and members of the court, let it be known that I choose as my successor my eldest son Malcolm, from now on to be called the Prince of Cumberland. His will not be the only honor bestowed. All merit will be nobly rewarded. We'll travel from here to Macbeth's castle at Inverness, to strengthen our friendship.

Macbeth   Leave the rest to me. I'll ride ahead and delight my wife with the news of your coming. [*He bows*] I humbly take my leave.

Duncan   My worthy Cawdor!

Macbeth   [*To himself*] The Prince of Cumberland! That's an obstacle that will trip me up unless I leap over it. It lies in my

50   For in my way it lies. Stars, hide your fires!
    Let not light see my black and deep desires:
    The eye wink at the hand; yet let that be
    Which the eye fears, when it is done, to see.

[*Exit*]

Duncan   True, worthy Banquo; he is full so valiant,
55   And in his commendations I am fed:
    It is a banquet to me. Let's after him,
    Whose care is gone before to bid us welcome:
    It is a peerless kinsman.

[*Flourish. Exeunt*]

Scene 5

Inverness. Macbeth's castle. Enter **Lady Macbeth**, *reading a letter.*

Lady Macbeth   'They met me in the day of success; and I have
learned by the perfect'st report, they have more in them than
mortal knowledge. When I burned in desire to question them
further, they made themselves air, into which they vanished.
5   Whiles I stood rapt in the wonder of it, came missives from
the king, who all-hailed me, 'Thane of Cawdor', by which
title, before, these Weird Sisters saluted me, and referred me
to the coming on of time, with 'Hail, king that shalt be!' This
have I thought good to deliver thee, my dearest partner of
10 greatness, that thou mightst not lose the due of rejoicing, by
being ignorant of what greatness is promised thee. Lay it to
thy heart, and farewell.'

way. Stars, stop shining! Let darkness hide my wicked ambitions! The work the hand must do is not for the eye to see. But what the eye fears has got to be done!

[*He goes*]

Duncan   [*To* **Banquo**, *nodding agreement*] True, worthy Banquo. He's so valiant. His worthiness is meat and drink to me, as good as a banquet. Let's follow him. He went ahead, thinking of our welfare, to prepare a welcome. He is a kinsman without equal.

[*Fanfare. They go*]

Scene 5

Macbeth's *castle at Inverness.* **Lady Macbeth** *enters, reading a letter from her husband.*

Lady Macbeth   "They met me on the day of victory. I have the strongest evidence that they possess supernatural powers. When I wanted to question them further, they turned into air and vanished. While I stood there in amazement, messengers came from the king, greeting me as Thane of Cawdor, the title with which these Weird Sisters had addressed me before. They foretold the future too, with 'Hail, king that shall be!' I am sending you this news, my dearest partner in greatness, so that you won't lose a moment's enjoyment through ignorance of the greatness that's in store for you. Keep this to yourself, and farewell."

Glamis thou art, and Cawdor; and shalt be
15　What thou art promised: yet do I fear thy nature;
It is too full o'th' milk of human kindness
To catch the nearest way: thou wouldst be great;
Art not without ambition, but without
The illness should attend it: what thou wouldst highly,
20　That wouldst thou holily; wouldst not play false,
And yet wouldst wrongly win: thou'ldst have, great Glamis,
That which cries 'Thus thou must do', if thou have it,
And that which rather thou dost fear to do
Than wishest should be undone. Hie thee thither,
25　That I may pour my spirits in thine ear,
And chastise with the valour of my tongue
All that impedes thee from the golden round,
Which fate and metaphysical aid doth seem
To have thee crowned withal.

[*Enter a* **Messenger**]

What is your tiding?

30　**Messenger**　The king comes here to-night.

Lady Macbeth　　　　　　　　　Thou'rt mad to say it!
Is not thy master with him? who, were't so,
Would have informed for preparation.

Messenger　So please you, it is true: our thane is coming:
One of my fellows had the speed of him;
35　Who, almost dead for breath, had scarcely more
Than would make up his message.

Lady Macbeth　　　　　　　　　Give him tending;
He brings great news. [**Messenger** *goes*] The raven himself
　　is hoarse
That croaks the fatal entrance of Duncan
Under my battlements. Come, you spirits

Thane of Glamis, and now of Cawdor. You shall be what you have been promised. Yet I'm worried about your nature. You are too tenderhearted to take shortcuts. You want greatness. You are not without ambition. But you lack the ruthlessness that's needed. You want high office by righteous means. You don't want to cheat, but you'd win unfairly. Great Glamis, you desire what calls for a great deed – yet you are too scared to do it, even though you want it to happen. Come home quickly, so that I can inspire you with my passion. My brave words will overcome the scruples standing between you and the golden circle – the crown that fate and the supernatural seem to have destined for you!

[*A* **Messenger** *enters*]

What's your news?

Messenger   The king comes here tonight.

Lady Macbeth   You're mad to say so. Isn't your master with him? If so, he would have warned us to get things ready.

Messenger   With respect, it's true. Our thane is coming. A fellow messenger ran ahead of him. Almost dead from exhaustion, he'd just enough breath to deliver his message.

Lady Macbeth   Look after him. He brings great news.

[*The* **Messenger** *leaves*]

That messenger of death, the raven, is hoarse from croaking the news of Duncan's fatal arrival here. Come, you spirits that

40   That tend on mortal thoughts, unsex me here,
        And fill me from the crown to the toe top-full
        Of direst cruelty! make thick my blood;
        Stop up th'access and passage to remorse,
        That no compunctious visitings of nature
45   Shake my fell purpose, nor keep peace between
        The effect and it! Come to my woman's breasts,
        And take my milk for gall, you murdering ministers,
        Wherever in your sightless substances
        You wait on nature's mischief! Come, thick night,
50   And pall thee in the dunnest smoke of hell,
        That my keen knife see not the wound it makes,
        Nor heaven peep through the blanket of the dark,
        To cry 'Hold, hold!'

        [*Enter* **Macbeth**]

                            Great Glamis! worthy Cawdor!
        Greater than both, by the all-hail hereafter!
55   Thy letters have transported me beyond
        This ignorant present, and I feel now
        The future in the instant.

Macbeth   My dearest love,
        Duncan comes here to-night.

Lady Macbeth   And when goes hence?

Macbeth   To-morrow, as he purposes.

Lady Macbeth   O, never
60   Shall sun that morrow see!
        Your face, my thane, is as a book where men
        May read strange matters. To beguile the time,
        Look like the time; bear welcome in your eye.
        Your hand, your tongue: look like the innocent flower,
65   But be the serpent under't. He that's coming

serve the thoughts of mortals: rid me of the natural
tenderness of my sex and fill me from head to toe with direst
cruelty! Thicken my blood. Make me remorseless, so that no
urgings of conscience can alter my foul plans, nor stand in the
way of what must be done. Come to my woman's breasts and
turn my milk sour, you ministers of murder, wherever you lurk
invisibly, awaiting evil deeds! Come, dark night, and shroud
yourself in the blackest smoke of Hell, so my sharp knife won't
see the wound it makes, nor will Heaven – peeping through
the blanket of darkness – cry, "Stop! Stop!"

[**Macbeth** *enters*]

Great Glamis! Worthy Cawdor! Greater even than both, by the
prophecy on the heath! Your letters have shown me the future
so clearly that I feel it with us now.

Macbeth   My dearest love, Duncan comes here tonight.

Lady Macbeth   And when does he go?

Macbeth   Tomorrow. Or so he intends . . .

Lady Macbeth   He'll never see tomorrow's sun! Your face, my
thane, is like a book. It can reveal strange things to its readers.
Avoid suspicion by acting normally. Be full of welcome in your
eye, your hand, your tongue. Look like the innocent flower,
but be the snake that's lying under it. Our guest must be taken

Must be provided for: and you shall put
This night's great business into my dispatch,
Which shall to all our nights and days to come
Give solely sovereign sway and masterdom.

Macbeth   We will speak further.

70 **Lady Macbeth**   Only look up clear:
To alter favour ever is to fear:
Leave all the rest to me.

[*Exeunt*]

Scene 6

Enter **King Duncan, Malcolm, Donalbain, Banquo, Lennox,
Macduff, Ross, Angus,** *and* **Attendants**.

Duncan   This castle hath a pleasant seat; the air
Nimbly and sweetly recommends itself
Unto our gentle senses.

Banquo   This guest of summer,
The temple-haunting martlet, does approve,
5   By his loved mansionry, that the heaven's breath
Smells wooingly here: no jutty, frieze,
Buttress, nor coign of vantage, but this bird
Hath made his pendent bed and procreant cradle:
Where they most breed and haunt, I have observed
10 The air is delicate.

[*Enter* **Lady Macbeth**]

care of. Tonight's great business you must leave to me. It will secure us unchallenged power for the rest of our lives.

Macbeth   We must discuss this more.

Lady Macbeth   Look frank and innocent. To show your feelings is dangerous. Leave everything else to me.

[*They go*]

Scene 6

Outside **Macbeth's** *castle.* **King Duncan, Malcolm, Donalbain, Banquo, Lennox, Macduff, Ross, Angus,** *and* **Attendants** *enter.*

Duncan   This castle is pleasantly situated. The sweet and clear air appeals to me.

Banquo   The scent must be attractive. In summertime, the swallows usually haunt our churches, but they've chosen to build their nests here. There's not a projection, buttress or convenient corner that's not been used for nesting and hatching by this bird. I've noticed that wherever they most live and breed, the air is delicate.

[**Lady Macbeth** *enters*]

Duncan   See, see! our honoured hostess!
The love that follows us sometime is our trouble,
Which still we thank as love. Herein I teach you
How you shall bid God 'ild us for your pains,
And thank us for your trouble.

Lady Macbeth   All our service
15   In every point twice done and then done double,
Were poor and single business to contend
Against those honours deep and broad, wherewith
Your majesty loads our house: for those of old,
And the late dignities heaped up to them,
We rest your hermits.

20 **Duncan**   Where's the thane of Cawdor?
We coursed him at the heels, and had a purpose
To be his purveyor: but he rides well,
And his great love (sharp as his spur) hath holp him
To his home before us. Fair and noble hostess,
We are your guest to-night.

25 **Lady Macbeth**   Your servants ever
Have theirs, themselves, and what is theirs, in compt,
To make their audit at your highness' pleasure,
Still to return your own.

Duncan   Give me your hand:
Conduct me to mine host; we love him highly,
30   And shall continue our graces towards him.
By your leave, hostess.

                                        [*Exeunt*]

Duncan   Look – our honored hostess! Tiresome though our subjects' love can sometimes be, we do appreciate it. This explains the present inconvenience. It proves our high regard for you.

Lady Macbeth   If what we did for you could be twice done, then doubled again, it would be a trifle compared with the great honors you have bestowed upon our family. For past favors, and the newest honors added to them, our lives are at your service.

Duncan   Where's the thane of Cawdor? We raced after him, intending to get here first. But he rides well, and his great love – sharp as his spur – has helped him to arrive before us. Fair and noble hostess, we are your guest tonight.

Lady Macbeth   Ourselves, our servants and all that we possess are yours to command.

Duncan   Give me your hand. Take me to our host. We love him greatly and shall continue to favor him. [*He offers her his hand*] May I, madam?

[*They go*]

Scene 7

Macbeth's castle. Enter a **sewer** *directing divers servants. Then enter* **Macbeth**.

Macbeth   If it were done, when 'tis done, then 'twere well
It were done quickly: if th' assassination
Could trammel up the consequence, and catch,
With his surcease, success; that but this blow
5   Might be the be-all and the end-all here,
But here, upon this bank and shoal of time,
We'd jump the life to come. But in these cases
We still have judgement here: that we but teach
Blood instructions, which being taught return
10   To plague th'inventor: this even-handed justice
Commends th'ingredience of our poisoned chalice
To our own lips. He's here in double trust:
First, as I am his kinsman and his subject,
Strong both against the deed: then, as his host,
15   Who should against his murderer shut the door,
Not bear the knife myself. Besides, this Duncan
Hath borne his faculties so meek, hath been
So clear in his great office, that his virtues
Will plead like angels, trumpet-tongued, against
20   The deep damnation of his taking-off;
And pity, like a naked new-born babe,
Striding the blast, or Heaven's cherubin, horsed
Upon the sightless couriers of the air,
Shall blow the horrid deed in every eye,
25   That tears shall drown the wind. I have no spur
To prick the sides of my intent, but only
Vaulting ambition, which o'erleaps itself,
And falls on th'other –

Scene 7

A room in **Macbeth's** *castle. A* **Butler** *and several* **Waiters** *cross, carrying dishes of food. Then* **Macbeth** *enters. He is thinking about the proposed murder of* **King Duncan***.*

Macbeth   If we could get away with the deed after it's done, then the quicker it were done, the better. If the murder had no consequences, and his death ensured success . . . If, when I strike the blow, that would be the end of it – here, right here, on this side of eternity – we'd willingly chance the life to come. But usually, we get what's coming to us here on earth. We teach the art of bloodshed, then become the victims of our own lessons. This evenhanded justice makes us swallow our own poison. [*Pause*] Duncan is here on double trust: first, because I'm his kinsman and his subject (both good arguments against the deed); then, because I'm his host, who should protect him from his murderer – not bear the knife. Besides, this Duncan has used his power so gently, he's been so incorruptible in his great office, that his virtues will plead like angels, their tongues trumpeting the damnable horror of his murder. And pity, like a naked newborn babe or Heaven's avenging angels riding the winds, will cry the deed to everyone so that tears will blind the eye. I've nothing to spur me on but high-leaping ambition, which can often bring about one's downfall.

[*Enter* **Lady Macbeth**]

How now! what news?

Lady Macbeth   He has almost supped: why have you left
the chamber?

Macbeth   Hath he asked for me?

30 **Lady Macbeth**   Know you not he has?

Macbeth   We will proceed no further in this business:
He hath honoured me of late, and I have bought
Golden opinions from all sorts of people,
Which would be worn now in their newest gloss,
35   Not cast aside so soon.

Lady Macbeth   Was the hope drunk
Wherein you dressed yourself? hath it slept since?
And wakes it now, to look so green and pale
At what it did so freely? From this time
Such I account thy love. Art thou afeard
40   To be the same in thine own act and valour
As thou art in desire? Wouldst thou have that
Which thou esteem'st the ornament of life,
And live a coward in thine own esteem,
Letting 'I dare not' wait upon 'I would',
Like the poor cat i'th'adage?

45 **Macbeth**   Prithee, peace:
I dare do all that may become a man;
Who dares do more is none.

Lady Macbeth   What beast was't then
That made you break this enterprise to me?
When you durst do it, then you were a man;
50   And, to be more than what you were, you would
Be so much more the man. Nor time nor place

[**Lady Macbeth** *enters*]

Well, what news?

Lady Macbeth   He's almost finished supper. Why have you left the room?

Macbeth   Has he asked for me?

Lady Macbeth   Don't you know he has?

Macbeth   We'll go no further in this business. He has honored me recently, and I've won great respect from all sorts of people. This is to be enjoyed while it's new, not cast aside so soon.

Lady Macbeth   [*Scornfully*] Was the hope drunk that made you determined before? Has it been sleeping since? And has it woken up to look queasily upon what it did when tipsy? From now on, I know what your love's worth. Are you afraid to match your acts with your ambitions? Can you want that glittering prize – the crown – yet be a self-confessed coward: "I'd like to, but I daren't," like the poor cat in the proverb that wanted fish but wouldn't get its feet wet?

Macbeth   That's enough of that! I'll dare do anything that's worthy of a man. Who dares do more isn't human.

Lady Macbeth   What monster was it then that made you share this scheme with me? When you dared to do it, then you were a man. To have ambition is to be so much more the man. Before, neither the time nor the place mattered – yet you were

Did then adhere, and yet you would make both:
They have made themselves, and that their fitness now
Does unmake you. I have given suck, and know
55 How tender 'tis to love the babe that milks me –
I would, while it was smiling in my face,
Have plucked my nipple from his boneless gums,
And dashed the brains out, had I so sworn as you
Have done to this.

Macbeth   If we should fail?

Lady Macbeth   We fail?
60 But screw your courage to the sticking place,
And we'll not fail. When Duncan is asleep –
Whereto the rather shall his day's hard journey
Soundly invite him – his two chamberlains
Will I with wine and wassail so convince,
65 That memory, the warder of the brain,
Shall be a fume, and the receipt of reason
A limbec only: when in swinish sleep
Their drenched natures lie as in a death,
What cannot you and I perform upon
70 Th'unguarded Duncan? what not put upon
His spongy officers, who shall bear the guilt
Of our great quell?

Macbeth   Bring forth men-children only!
For thy undaunted mettle should compose
Nothing but males. Will it not be received,
75 When we have marked with blood those sleepy two
Of his own chamber, and used their very daggers,
That they have done't?

Lady Macbeth   Who dares receive it other,
As we shall make our griefs and clamour roar
Upon his death?

prepared to arrange them both. Now they have arranged themselves, and at this perfect opportunity you've lost your nerve. I've suckled babies. I know how tender it is to love the child at my breast. While it was smiling up at me, I'd have pulled my nipple from its mouth and dashed its brains out, if I'd sworn – as you have sworn – to do it.

Macbeth   What if we should fail?

Lady Macbeth   We fail? Just screw up your courage to the uttermost, and we won't fail. When Duncan is asleep – and he'll sleep soundly after his hard day's journey – I'll ply his two officers with so much drink their memories will be fogged and their brains addled. When they are drunk and sleeping like pigs, what can't we do to the unguarded Duncan? What can't we blame on his sodden officers? They'll get the blame for our great murder.

Macbeth   Be mother to male children only! Your dauntless spirit should create nothing but males! Won't everyone assume, after we've smeared those two sleepy guards with blood – and even used their very daggers! – that they have done it?

Lady Macbeth   Who would dare to take it otherwise since we shall grieve and lament his death so loudly?

Macbeth   I am settled, and bend up
80   Each corporal agent to this terrible feat.
      Away, and mock the time with fairest show:
      False face must hide what the false heart doth know.

                                                    [*Exeunt*]

Macbeth   I'm settled on it then. All my faculties shall be devoted to this terrible deed. Let's go and pass the time as perfect hosts. We must conceal our false hearts behind false faces.

[*They go*]

Act two

Scene 1

*Macbeth's castle, a few hours later. Enter **Banquo**, and **Fleance** with a torch before him.*

Banquo How goes the night, boy?

Fleance   The moon is down;
    I have not heard the clock.

Banquo And she goes down at twelve.

Fleance   I take't, 'tis later, sir.

Banquo Hold, take my sword. There's husbandry in heaven,
5   Their candles are all out. Take thee that too.
    A heavy summons lies like lead upon me,
    And yet I would not sleep. Merciful powers,
    Restrain in me the cursed thoughts that nature
    Gives way to in repose! Give me my sword.
10   Who's there?

[*Enter **Macbeth**, and a **Servant** with a torch.*]

Macbeth A friend.

Banquo What, sir, not yet at rest? The king's a-bed.
    He hath been in unusual pleasure, and
    Sent forth great largess to your offices.
15   This diamond he greets your wife withal,
    By the name of most kind hostess; and shut up
    In measureless content.

Act two

Scene 1

A few hours later, in a courtyard in **Macbeth's** *castle.* **Banquo** *enters with his son* **Fleance**, *who is carrying a torch.*

Banquo   What time is it, my boy?

Fleance   [*Looking at the sky*] The moon's gone down. I haven't heard the clock.

Banquo   The moon goes down at midnight.

Fleance   I think it's later than that, sir.

Banquo   Here, take my sword. [*He fumbles in the dark*] They must be penny-pinching in heaven. They've snuffed out the stars! [*He undoes his belt and dagger*] Take these as well. [*He yawns*] My eyes are as heavy as lead, but I'm afraid to sleep. [*He shudders*] God, take away the evil thoughts that come to me in dreams. [*He hears a noise*] Give me my sword again. Who's there?

[**Macbeth** *enters with a* **Servant**]

Macbeth   A friend.

Banquo   [*Lowering his weapon*] What, sir? Still up? The king's in bed. He's been in high spirits. He has tipped the servants well. He wants to give your wife this diamond for being such a kind hostess. He retired very happy.

Macbeth   Being unprepared,
Our will became the servant to defect,
Which else should free have wrought.

Banquo   All's well.
20 I dreamt last night of the three Weird Sisters:
To you they have showed some truth.

Macbeth   I think not of them:
Yet, when we can entreat an hour to serve,
We would spend it in some words upon that business,
If you would grant the time.

Banquo   At your kind'st leisure.

25 **Macbeth** If you shall cleave to my consent, when 'tis,
It shall make honour for you.

Banquo   So I lose none
In seeking to augment it, but still keep
My bosom franchised and allegiance clear,
I shall be counselled.

Macbeth   Good repose the while!

30 **Banquo** Thanks, sir: the like to you!

         [Exeunt **Banquo** *and* **Fleance**]

Macbeth Go bid thy mistress, when my drink is ready,
She strike upon the bell. Get thee to bed.

          [Exit **Servant**]

Is this a dagger which I see before me,
The handle toward my hand? Come, let me clutch thee.
35 I have thee not, and yet I see thee still.
Art thou not, fatal vision, sensible
To feeling as to sight? or art thou but

Macbeth   We weren't expecting him. We did the best we could.

Banquo   It was splendid. [*Changing the subject*] I dreamed of the three Weird Sisters last night. In your case they've been pretty accurate.

Macbeth   [*Lightly*] I haven't given them a thought. But one day when you've got some time to spare we must talk about their prophecies.

Banquo   At your service.

Macbeth   Back me when the time comes, and you'll do yourself some good.

Banquo   Provided I can remain honorable in doing so, free from evil and loyal to the king, I'm open to your advice.

Macbeth   Sleep well meanwhile!

Banquo   Thanks, sir. And the same to you!

[**Banquo** *and* **Fleance** *leave*]

Macbeth   [*To his* **Servant**] Tell your mistress to ring the bell when my drink's ready; then you get to bed.

[*The* **Servant** *goes.* **Macbeth** *sits deep in thought at a table. Then he comes to, startled, but staring into space*]

Is this a dagger I see before me? With its handle toward my hand? [*Speaking to it*] Come – let me hold you! [*He snatches at the empty air*] Nothing there. Yet I can still see you. Can't you be felt as well as seen? Or are you just an imaginary

A dagger of the mind, a false creation,
Proceeding from the heat-oppressed brain?
40   I see thee yet, in form as palpable
As this which now I draw.
Thou marshall'st me the way that I was going,
And such an instrument I was to use!
Mine eyes are made the fools o'th'other senses,
45   Or else worth all the rest: I see thee still;
And on thy blade and dudgeon gouts of blood,
Which was not so before. There's no such thing:
It is the bloody business which informs
Thus to mine eyes. Now o'er the one half-world
50   Nature seems dead, and wicked dreams abuse
The curtained sleep; now witchcraft celebrates
Pale Hecate's off'rings; and withered Murder,
Alarumed by his sentinel, the wolf,
Whose howl's his watch, thus with his stealthy pace,
55   With Tarquin's ravishing strides, towards his design
Moves like a ghost. Thou sure and firm-set earth,
Hear not my steps, which way they walk, for fear
Thy very stones prate of my whereabout,
And take the present horror from the time,
60   Which now suits with it. Whiles I threat, he lives:
Words to the heat of deeds too cold breath gives.

[*A bell rings*]

I go, and it is done: the bell invites me.
Hear it not, Duncan, for it is a knell
That summons thee to heaven, or to hell.

[*Exit*]

dagger? The invention of a sick mind? [*He closes his eyes, then looks again*] Still there! And [*taking his own dagger from its sheath*] looking just as solid as the one I'm drawing now. [*Excitedly*] It's pointing the way I meant to go, and a dagger *was* my chosen weapon! [*Doubt creeps in*] My eyes could be fooling me. [*More confidently*] More likely, they're worth all my other senses put together. [*He blinks hard*] Still there! With clots of blood on the blade and handle that weren't there before! [*He covers his eyes*] It must be all imaginary. I'm so obsessed with murder that I'm seeing things. Half the world's asleep. Wicked dreams invade men's minds. Witches perform their rites. Howling wolves wake murderers, who stalk their victims lustfully and glide upon them like ghosts. [*He makes up his mind*] My footsteps must be silent on the telltale earth. I mustn't give myself away, just when the time is ripe to do the deed. All this ranting only lengthens his life. Too much talk cools one's courage.

[*A bell rings*]

Now I'll go, and it's as good as done. The bell is my invitation. Do not hear it, Duncan! It's a bell that summons you to heaven – or to hell!

[*He stealthily heads for* **Duncan's** *bedroom*]

Scene 2

Lady Macbeth *enters*.

Lady Macbeth   That which hath made them drunk hath made
      me bold:
   What hath quenched them hath given me fire. Hark! Peace!
   It was the owl that shrieked, the fatal bellman,
   Which gives the stern'st good-night. He is about it:
5   The doors are open; and the surfeited grooms
   Do mock their charge with snores: I have drugged their
      possetts,
   That death and nature do contend about them,
   Whether they live or die.

Macbeth   Who's there? what, ho!

Lady Macbeth   Alack! I am afraid they have awaked,
10   And 'tis not done: th'attempt and not the deed
   Confounds us. Hark! I laid their daggers ready,
   He could not miss 'em. Had he not resembled
   My father as he slept, I had done't.

[*Enter* **Macbeth**]

                                  My husband!

Macbeth   I have done the deed. Didst thou not hear a noise?

15 **Lady Macbeth**   I heard the owl scream, and the crickets cry.
   Did you not speak?

Macbeth   When?

Lady Macbeth   Now.

Macbeth   As I descended?

Lady Macbeth   Ay.

Scene 2

Lady Macbeth *enters, carrying a goblet.*

Lady Macbeth   The wine that has made them drunk has made me brave. The drink that has put out their fire has lighted mine. [*Pause*] Listen. Ssh! An owl shrieked; the announcer of death, which says good night so sternly. [*Thinking of Macbeth*] He's doing it now. The bedroom doors are open, and the drunken servants are snoring. I've drugged their drinks. They're midway between life and death.

Macbeth   [*Calling from upstairs*] Who's there? Hey!

Lady Macbeth   Oh no! They have have wakened, and it isn't done. We'll be ruined if we've bungled it. Ssh! [*She pauses, listening*] I left the daggers ready. He couldn't miss them. If Duncan hadn't looked like my father in his sleep, I'd have done it myself.

[**Macbeth** *staggers in, carrying two daggers, his hands and arms bathed in blood*]

Lady Macbeth   My husband!

Macbeth   [*In a low voice*] The deed is done. Didn't you hear a noise?

Lady Macbeth   I heard an owl scream and some crickets cry. [*They listen*] Didn't you speak?

Macbeth   When?

Lady Macbeth   Now.

Macbeth   As I came down?

Lady Macbeth   Yes.

Macbeth   Hark!
Who lies i'th' second chamber?

Lady Macbeth   Donalbain.

20 **Macbeth**   This is a sorry sight.

Lady Macbeth   A foolish thought, to say a sorry sight.

Macbeth   There's one did laugh in's sleep, and one cried
'Murder!'
That they did wake each other: I stood and heard them:
But they did say their prayers, and addressed them
Again to sleep.

25 **Lady Macbeth**   There are two lodged together.

Macbeth   One cried 'God bless us!' and 'Amen' the other,
As they had seen me with these hangman's hands:
List'ning their fear, I could not say 'Amen',
When they did say 'God bless us'.

30 **Lady Macbeth**   Consider it not so deeply.

Macbeth   But wherefore could not I pronounce 'Amen'?
I had most need of blessing, and 'Amen'
Stuck in my throat.

Lady Macbeth   These deeds must not be thought
After these ways; so, it will make us mad.

35 **Macbeth**   Methought I heard a voice cry 'Sleep no more!
Macbeth does murder sleep', the innocent sleep,
Sleep that knits up the ravelled sleave of care,
The death of each day's life, sore labour's bath,
Balm of hurt minds, great Nature's second course,
Chief nourisher in life's feast, –

40 **Lady Macbeth**   What do you mean?

Macbeth   Still it cried 'Sleep no more!' to all the house:

Macbeth   Listen! [*They are both silent*] Who's in the second bedroom?

Lady Macbeth   Donalbain.

Macbeth   [*Looking at his hands*] This is a dreadful sight.

Lady Macbeth   [*Scornfully*] "A dreadful sight" – that's stupid!

Macbeth   [*Disregarding her*] One of them laughed in his sleep, and one cried "Murder!" So they woke each other up. I stood and heard them. But they only said their prayers and went to sleep again.

Lady Macbeth   [*Explaining*] There are two in that room – Malcolm and Donalbain.

Macbeth   One cried, "God bless us!" and the other one said, "Amen" – as though they'd seen me with these executioner's hands. Hearing them so scared, I couldn't say, "Amen," when they said, "God bless us" . . .

Lady Macbeth   Don't brood so much!

Macbeth   But why couldn't I say, "Amen"? I needed the blessing most, but "Amen" stuck in my throat!

Lady Macbeth   We mustn't keep thinking about it like this; it will drive us mad.

Macbeth   I thought I heard a voice crying, "Sleep no more! Macbeth has murdered sleep!" [*He goes on thoughtfully*] Innocent sleep! Sleep that relieves all our worries. The natural end of every day. The soothing bath for weary workers. The balm for disturbed minds. The rejuvenator of life. The main course in life's feast –

Lady Macbeth   What do you mean?

Macbeth   [*Ignoring her*] Still the voice cried, "Sleep no more!"

       'Glamis hath murdered sleep, and therefore Cawdor
       Shall sleep no more: Macbeth shall sleep no more!'

Lady Macbeth   Who was it that thus cried? Why,
       worthy thane,
45   You do unbend your noble strength, to think
       So brainsickly of things. Go get some water,
       And wash this filthy witness from your hand.
       Why did you bring these daggers from the place?
       They must lie there: go carry them, and smear
50   The sleepy grooms with blood.

Macbeth   I'll go no more:
       I am afraid to think what I have done;
       Look on't again I dare not.

Lady Macbeth   Infirm of purpose!
       Give me the daggers: the sleeping and the dead
       Are but as pictures: 'tis the eye of childhood
55   That fears a painted devil. If he do bleed,
       I'll gild the faces of the grooms withal,
       For it must seem their guilt.

                          [She exits. Knocking within]

Macbeth   Whence is that knocking?
       How is't with me, when every noise appals me?
       What hands are here? ha! they pluck out mine eyes!
60   Will all great Neptune's ocean wash this blood
       Clean from my hand? No; this my hand will rather
       The multitudinous seas incarnadine,
       Making the green one red.

[Lady Macbeth *returns.*]

Lady Macbeth   My hands are of your colour; but I shame
65   To wear a heart so white. [*Knocking*] I hear a knocking

to all the house. "Lord Glamis has murdered sleep, and so Lord Cawdor shall sleep no more – Macbeth shall sleep no more!"

Lady Macbeth   Who cried like that? Why, my lord, you'll wear yourself out, thinking about things so dementedly. Go and get some water. Wash that filthy evidence off your hands. Why did you bring the daggers with you? They must be left up there. Take them back, and smear the sleepy servants with blood.

Macbeth   [*Horrified*] I won't go back! I'm afraid to think of what I've done. I daren't look at it again!

Lady Macbeth   Coward! Give me the daggers! Sleeping and dead people are like pictures of themselves. Only children fear a picture, even of the devil. If he's still bleeding, I'll smear the faces of the servants so it will look as if they did it.

[**Lady Macbeth** *goes out. There are sounds of knocking*]

Macbeth   Where's that knocking? What's happened to me, that every noise scares me? [*Looking down*] Whose hands are these? They're plucking my eyes out! [*Groaning*] Is there enough water in the oceans to wash my hands of this blood? No! More likely my hands will stain the vast green seas blood-red.

[**Lady Macbeth** *returns. Her hands are red with blood*]

Lady Macbeth   My hands are the same color as yours – but I'd be ashamed to have a heart as white as yours! [*There is more knocking*] I can hear someone knocking at the South Gate.

At the south entry: retire we to our chamber:
A little water clears us of this deed:
How easy is it then! Your constancy
Hath left you unattended. [*Knocking*] Hark! more knocking.
70   Get on your nightgown, lest occasion call us
And show us to be watchers: be not lost
So poorly in your thoughts.

Macbeth   To know my deed, 'twere best not know myself.
[*Knocking*]
Wake Duncan with thy knocking! I would thou couldst!

[*Exeunt*]

Scene 3

Knocking within. Enter a **Porter**.

Porter   Here's a knocking indeed! If a man were porter of
hell-gate, he should have old turning the key. [*Knocking*]
Knock, knock, knock! Who's there, i'th' name of Beelzebub?
Here's a farmer, that hanged himself on th'expectation of
5   plenty: come in, time-server; have napkins enow about you;
here you'll sweat for't. [*Knocking*] Knock, knock! Who's
there, in th'other devil's name? Faith, here's an equivocator,
that could swear in both the scales against either scale, who
committed treason enough for God's sake, yet could not
10   equivocate to heaven: O, come in, equivocator. [*Knocking*]
Knock, knock, knock! Who's there? Faith, here's an English
tailor come hither, for stealing out of a French hose: come in,
tailor, here you may roast your goose. [*Knocking*] Knock,
knock! never at quiet! What are you? But this place is too cold

Let's return to our bedroom. A little water will wash away all traces of the deed. Then it will be easy. [*Scornfully*] You've lost your nerve! [*Knocking*] Listen – more knocking. Put on your nightgown, in case we're called, and seen to be out of bed. And don't get so lost in thought!

Macbeth   Better to be lost in thought than face reality. [*The knocking continues. He shudders*] Wake Duncan with your knocking! I wish you could!

[*They leave together*]

Scene 3

The main gate of **Macbeth**'*s Castle. The* **Porter** *enters. He has heard the knocking, but he has drunk far too much to be steady on his feet.*

Porter   There's knocking for you! Now if I were the porter at the gate of hell, I'd be forever unlocking the door! [*He pretends that he is hell's porter*] Knock, knock, knock! Who's there, in the devil's name? [*Guessing*] Perhaps it's a farmer who hanged himself when corn was cheap. Come in, speculator! Bring enough handkerchiefs with you – here you'll have to sweat it out! [*Knocking*] Knock, knock! Who's there, in the name of Satan? [*Another guess*] Faith, here's one of these devil's advocates, who could take any side in an argument and tell any number of lies for God's sake – but who couldn't talk his way into heaven! Oh, come in, twister! [*Knocking*] Knock, knock, knock! Who's there? [*Guessing yet again*] Faith, here's an English tailor, who's come here for stealing cloth – from breeches! Come in, tailor! You can heat your iron here! [*Knocking*] Knock, knock! No peace. Who are you? [*The cold gets too much for him; he slaps his arms*] But this place is too cold for hell. I'll be a devil-porter no longer. I'd planned to let in

75

15   for hell. I'll devil-porter it no further: I had thought to have
      let in some of all professions, that go the primrose way to
      th'everlasting bonfire. [*Knocking*] Anon, anon! I pray you,
      remember the porter. [*Opens the gate*]

      [*Enter* **Macduff** *and* **Lennox**]

      Macduff   Was it so late, friend, ere you went to bed,
20   That you do lie so late?

      Porter   Faith, sir, we were carousing till the second cock: and
      drink, sir, is a great provoker of three things.

      Macduff   What three things does drink especially provoke?

      Porter   Marry, sir, nose-painting, sleep, and urine. Lechery,
25   sir, it provokes and unprovokes: it provokes the desire, but it
      takes away the performance. Therefore, much drink may be
      said to be an equivocator with lechery: it makes him, and it
      mars him; it sets him on, and it takes him off; it persuades
      him, and disheartens him; makes him stand to, and not stand
30   to: in conclusion, equivocates him in a sleep, and giving him
      the lie, leaves him.

      Macduff   I believe drink gave thee the lie last night.

      Porter   That it did, sir, i'the very throat on me: but I requited
      him for his lie, and, I think, being too strong for him, though
35   he took up my legs sometime, yet I made a shift to cast him.

      Macduff   Is thy master stirring?

      [*Enter* **Macbeth**]

      Our knocking has awaked him; here he comes.

      Lennox   Good-morrow, noble sir.

      Macbeth   Good-morrow, both.

some of all the professions . . . including those that go to hell the prim and proper way . . . [*Knocking*] All right, all right!

[*He unlocks the gate.* **Macduff** *and* **Lennox** *enter. He holds out his hand for a tip*]

Please remember the porter.

Macduff   [*Obliging*] Did you get to bed so late, my friend, that you overslept?

Porter   Well, sir, we were drinking till three o'clock in the morning. And drink, sir, is a great provoker of three things.

Macduff   What three things does drink especially provoke? [*Winking to* **Lennox**]

Porter   Well, sir: red noses, sleep and urine. Sex it turns on and turns off. It turns on the desire, but it turns off the performance. Therefore too much drink is a sort of double dealer with sex. It makes sex and spoils sex. It gives a man the urge and takes the urge away. It encourages him, then discourages him. It makes him rise to the occasion, then not rise to the occasion. Finally, it tricks him with a dream, and putting him down, it abandons him.

Macduff   I think drink put *you* down last night!

Porter   It did that, sir! It got me by the throat. But I got my revenge. Being too strong for it, maybe, I managed to "throw it up" even though it put me down!

[**Macbeth** *enters*]

Macduff   Is your master up? [*He sees* **Macbeth**] Our knocking has awakened him. Here he comes.

Lennox   Good morning, sir!

Macbeth   Good morning to you both.

40 **Macduff**   Is the king stirring, worthy thane?

Macbeth   Not yet.

Macduff   He did command me to call timely on him;
I have almost slipped the hour.

Macbeth   I'll bring you to him.

45 **Macduff**   I know this is a joyful trouble to you;
But yet 'tis one.

Macbeth   The labour we delight in physics pain.
This is the door.

Macduff   I'll make so bold to call,
50 For 'tis my limited service.

[*Exit*]

Lennox   Goes the king hence to-day?

Macbeth   He does: he did appoint so.

Lennox   The night has been unruly: where we lay,
Our chimneys were blown down, and, as they say,
55 Lamentings heard i'th'air, strange screams of death,
And prophesying with accents terrible
Of dire combustion and confused events
New hatched to th'woeful time. The obscure bird
Clamoured the livelong night: some say, the earth
60 Was feverous and did shake.

Macbeth   'Twas a rough night.

Lennox   My young remembrance cannot parallel
A fellow to it.

[*Enter* **Macduff**]

Macduff   Is the king up, my lord?

Macbeth   Not yet.

Macduff   He ordered me to call him early. I'm almost late.

Macbeth   I'll take you to him. [*They walk toward the king's bedroom*]

Macduff   Hosting the king is an agreeable inconvenience to you, I know but it's an inconvenience none the less.

Macbeth   Tasks we like doing never seem irksome. [*Pointing*] This is the door.

Macduff   I'll risk a call. That's what I'm here for.

[**Macduff** *goes in*]

Lennox   Is the king leaving today?

Macbeth   He is. That was his plan.

Lennox   It's been a stormy night. Where we stayed, our chimneys were blown down. People said they heard wailing, strange screams of death, and terrible prophecies of revolution and disorder, all products of these troubled times. An owl screeched all night long. Some say there were earthquakes.

Macbeth   It was a rough night.

Lennox   I can't recall one like it in my short lifetime.

[**Macduff** *returns, wild-eyed*]

Macduff   O horror! horror! horror! Tongue, nor heart,
65   Cannot conceive nor name thee!

Macbeth, Lennox   What's the matter?

Macduff   Confusion now hath made his masterpiece!
   Most sacrilegious murder hath broke ope
   The Lord's anointed temple, and stole thence
70   The life o'th'building.

Macbeth   What is't you say? the life?

Lennox   Mean you his majesty?

Macduff   Approach the chamber, and destroy your sight
   With a new Gorgon: do not bid me speak;
75   See, and then speak yourselves.

                              [*Exeunt* **Macbeth** *and* **Lennox**]

                              Awake! awake!
   Ring the alarum bell! Murder and treason!
   Banquo and Donalbain! Malcolm! awake!
   Shake off this downy sleep, death's counterfeit,
80   And look on death itself! up, up, and see
   The great doom's image! Malcolm! Banquo!
   As from your graves rise up, and walk like sprites,
   To countenance this horror! Ring the bell. [*Bell rings*]

   [*Enter* **Lady Macbeth**]

Lady Macbeth   What's the business,
85   That such a hideous trumpet calls to parley
   The sleepers of the house? speak, speak!

Macduff   O, gentle lady,
   'Tis not for you to hear what I can speak:
   The repetition, in a woman's ear,
90   Would murder as it fell.

Macduff   Oh, horror, horror, horror! There are no words that can tell it – no mind able to conceive it.

Macbeth
}   What's the matter?
Lennox

Macduff   The greatest possible tragedy has taken place! God's anointed king has been murdered. Robbed of his sacred life!

Macbeth   What's that you say? His life?

Lennox   You mean His Majesty?

Macduff   Come to the bedroom. What you'll see will blind you and turn you to stone. Don't ask me to speak. See – then speak yourselves!

[**Macbeth** *and* **Lennox** *run off*]

Wake up! Wake up! Ring the alarm bell. Murder and treason! Banquo and Donalbain! Malcolm, wake up! Shake off your comforting sleep – death's imitator – and see death itself. Up, up, and see an image of Judgment Day. Malcolm! Banquo! Rise as if from your graves. Walk like ghosts to face this scene of horror! Ring the bell!

[*An alarm bell clangs.* **Lady Macbeth** *enters, all innocence*]

Lady Macbeth   What's the matter, that such a fearful alarm should summon our guests from sleep? Speak, speak!

Macduff   Oh, gentle lady, my words are not for your ears. No woman could survive the telling.

[*Enter* **Banquo**]

                    O Banquo! Banquo!
Our royal master's murdered!

Lady Macbeth   Woe, alas!
What, in our house?

95 **Banquo**   Too cruel, any where.
Dear Duff, I prithee, contradict thyself,
And say it is not so.

    [**Macbeth** *and* **Lennox** *return*]

Macbeth   Had I but died an hour before this chance,
I had lived a blessed time; for from this instant
100 There's nothing serious in mortality
All is but toys: renown and grace is dead,
The wine of life is drawn, and the mere lees
Is left this vault to brag of.

    [*Enter* **Malcolm** *and* **Donalbain**]

Donalbain   What is amiss?

105 **Macbeth**   You are, and do not know't:
The spring, the head, the fountain of your blood
Is stopped – the very source of it is stopped.

Macduff   Your royal father's murdered.

Malcolm   O, by whom?

110 **Lennox**   Those of his chamber, as it seemed, had done't:
Their hands and faces were all badged with blood,
So were their daggers, which unwiped we found
Upon their pillows:
They stared and were distracted, no man's life
115 Was to be trusted with them.

[**Banquo** *enters*]

Oh, Banquo, Banquo! The king has been murdered!

Lady Macbeth   Oh, no! What? In our house?

Banquo   It is too cruel, anywhere. Dear Duff, I beg you.
Contradict yourself. Say it isn't true!

[**Macbeth** *and* **Lennox** *return*]

Macbeth   If I had died an hour before this happened, I'd have
lived a blessed life span. From now on, there's nothing left
worth living for. Everything is a sham. Honor and dignity are
dead. The wine of life has gone. Only the dregs remain.

[**Malcolm** *and* **Donalbain,** *the king's sons, enter*]

Donalbain   What's the trouble?

Macbeth   Yours, but you don't know it. The spring, the source,
the fountainhead of your family has been stopped up.

Macduff   Your royal father has been murdered.

Malcolm   Oh, no. Who did it?

Lennox   By the look of things, his servants. Their hands and
faces were all smeared with blood. So were their daggers. We
found them on their pillows, still unwiped. They stared around
and looked dazed. No man's life was safe with them.

Macbeth   O, yet I do repent me of my fury,
That I did kill them.

Macduff   Wherefore did you so?

Macbeth   Who can be wise, amazed, temp'rate and furious,
120   Loyal and neutral, in a moment? no man:
Th'expedition of my violent love
Outrun the pauser, reason. Here lay Duncan,
His silver skin laced with his golden blood,
And his gashed stabs looked like a breach in nature
125   For ruin's wasteful entrance: there, the murderers,
Steeped in the colours of their trade, their daggers
Unmannerly breeched with gore: who could refrain,
That had a heart to love, and in that heart
Courage to make's love known?

130 **Lady Macbeth** [*Seeming to faint*]   Help me hence, ho!

Macduff   Look to the lady.

Malcolm   [*Aside*]   Why do we hold our tongues,
That most may claim this argument for ours?

Donalbain   What should be spoken here, where our fate,
135   Hid in an auger-hole, may rush and seize us?
Let's away.
Our tears are not yet brewed.

Malcolm   Nor our strong sorrow
Upon the foot of motion.

140 **Banquo**   Look to the lady.
And when we have our naked frailties hid,
That suffer in exposure, let us meet,
And question this most bloody piece of work,
To know it further. Fears and scruples shake us:
145   In the great hand of God I stand, and thence
Against the undivulged pretence I fight
Of treasonous malice.

Macbeth   Oh, how I wish now I hadn't lost my self-control and killed them!

Macduff   Why did you, then?

Macbeth   Who can be wise and astounded, calm and furious, loyal and neutral, all at the same time? Nobody. My passion overwhelmed my reason. Here lay Duncan – his white skin streaked with his precious blood, and his stab wounds obviously fatal. There were the murderers, steeped in the colors of their trade, their daggers dripping with blood. Who could hold back, that had a loving heart and the courage to show it?

Lady Macbeth   Help me, please. [*Pretending to faint*]

Macduff   Look after the lady.

Malcolm   [*To* **Donalbain**] Why are we silent, when it's our business more than anyone else's?

Donalbain   [*Replying*] What should we say here, where our own lives are in danger? Let's go. Our tears are not yet ready.

Malcolm   Nor is our deep sorrow fully felt.

Banquo   [*To* **Servants**] Take care of the lady. [*To the others*] We're catching cold. Let's get dressed, then meet to discuss this terrible murder and the motives behind it. Doubts and fears disturb us. I align myself with God. From that position I'm ready to fight against any secret plot or wicked treason!

Macduff   And so do I.

All   So all.

150 **Macbeth**   Let's briefly put on manly readiness.
     And meet i'th'hall together.

All   Well contented.

[*Exeunt all but* **Malcolm** *and* **Donalbain**]

Malcolm   What will you do? Let's not consort with them:
     To show an unfelt sorrow is an office
155   Which the false man does easy. I'll to England.

Donalbain   To Ireland, I: our separated fortune
     Shall keep us both the safer: where we are
     There's daggers in men's smiles: the near in blood,
     The nearer bloody.

160 **Malcolm**   This murderous shaft that's shot
     Hath not yet lighted, and our safest way
     Is to avoid the aim. Therefore to horse,
     And let us not be dainty of leave-taking,
     But shift away: there's warrant in that theft
165   Which steals itself when there's no mercy left.

[*Exeunt*]

Scene 4

Before Macbeth's castle. Enter **Ross** *with an* **Old Man**.

Old Man   Threescore and ten I can remember well,
     Within the volume of which time I have seen

Macduff   And so am I.

All   And all of us.

Macbeth   Let's quickly dress for action and meet in the hall.

All   Agreed.

[*They go, except for* **Malcolm** *and* **Donalbain**]

Malcolm   What will you do? Let's not mix with them. It's easy for a hypocrite to show sorrow he doesn't feel. I'll go to England.

Donalbain   Ireland for me. We'll be safer if we go our separate ways. Here, smilers have knives beneath their cloaks. Our closest relatives have most reason to murder us.

Malcolm   This murder is only the start. We should get out of the firing line. Let's ride off and not be too polite about leave-taking. Just slip away. Where there's no mercy, there's no shame in stealing off.

[*They go*]

Scene 4

Next morning, outside **Macbeth's** *castle.* **Ross** *and an* **Old Man** *enter.*

Old Man   In all my seventy years, I've seen some dreadful times

Hours dreadful and things strange; but this sore night
Hath trifled former knowings.

Ross   Ha, good father,
5   Thou seest the heavens, as troubled with man's act,
Threatens his bloody stage: by th' clock 'tis day,
And yet dark night strangles the travelling lamp:
Is't night's predominance, or the day's shame,
That darkness does the face of earth entomb,
10 When living light should kiss it?

Old Man   'Tis unnatural,
Even like the deed that's done. On Tuesday last
A falcon towering in her pride of place
Was by a mousing owl hawked at and killed.

Ross   And Duncan's horses – a thing most strange and
      certain –
15 Beauteous and swift, the minions of their race,
Turned wild in nature, broke their stalls, flung out,
Contending 'gainst obedience, as they would make
War with mankind.

Old Man   'Tis said they eat each other.

Ross   They did so, to th'amazement of mine eyes,
20 That looked upon't.

[*Enter* **Macduff**]

                              Here comes the good Macduff.
How goes the world, sir, now?

Macduff   Why, see you not?

Ross   Is't known who did this more than bloody deed?

Macduff   Those that Macbeth hath slain.

and some strange things. But compared with this awful night, they're insignificant.

Ross Ah, good father, the heavens are showing their displeasure at mankind's behavior! By the clock, it's day. Yet night still smothers the sun. Is the earth in darkness because the day is too ashamed to show its face?

Old Man It's most unnatural, just like the recent murder. Last Tuesday, a high-flying falcon was attacked and killed by a mouse-hunting owl.

Ross And this is strange but true: Duncan's horses, beautiful, swift creatures with fine pedigrees, suddenly went wild. They broke their stalls, kicked out, refusing to obey – as if they'd declared war on man.

Old Man It's said they ate each other.

Ross They did, too, to my amazement. I saw it!

[**Macduff** *enters*]

Here comes the good Macduff. How are things now, sir?

Macduff [*Pointing skyward at the weather*] Why, can't you see?

Ross Does anyone know who did this unspeakably bloody deed?

Macduff [*Cautiously*] The men Macbeth killed . . .

Ross   Alas, the day!
What good could they pretend?

Macduff   They were suborned.
25 Malcolm and Donalbain, the king's two sons,
Are stol'n away and fled, which puts upon them
Suspicion of the deed.

Ross   'Gainst nature still!
Thriftless ambition, that wilt ravin up
Thine own life's means! Then 'tis most like
30 The sovereignty will fall upon Macbeth.

Macduff   He is already named, and gone to Scone
To be invested.

Ross   Where is Duncan's body?

Macduff   Carried to Colmekill,
The sacred storehouse of his predecessors,
35 And guardian of their bones.

Ross   Will you to Scone?

Macduff   No cousin, I'll to Fife.

Ross   Well, I will thither.

Macduff   Well, may you see things well done there: adieu!
Lest our old robes sit easier than our new!

Ross   Farewell, father.

40 **Old Man**   God's benison go with you, and with those
That would make good of bad and friends of foes!

                                        [*Exeunt*]

Ross   A bad day! What could they hope to gain?

Macduff   They were hired. Malcolm and Donalbain, the king's two sons, have fled the country, an act which makes the thanes suspect them of the deed.

Ross   Another unnatural act. How carelessly ambition destroys itself! Then most likely Macbeth will become king?

Macduff   He's already been chosen and is at Scone for the coronation.

Ross   Where's Duncan's body?

Macduff   Taken to Iona, the family tomb.

Ross   Are you going to Scone?

Macduff   No, cousin. I'm going home to Fife.

Ross   Well, I'm going to Scone.

Macduff   Let us hope you'll see things well done there. Farewell. But things may have changed for the worse.

Ross   [*To the* **Old Man**] Farewell, father.

Old Man   God's blessing go with you and with all who try to make good of bad and friends of foes!

[*They go off in different directions*]

Act Three

Scene 1

The palace at Forres. **Banquo** *enters.*

Banquo   Thou hast it now, King, Cawdor, Glamis, all,
As the weird women promised, and I fear
Thou play'dst most foully for't: yet it was said
It should not stand in thy posterity,
5   But that myself should be the root and father
Of many kings. If there come truth from them –
As upon thee, Macbeth, their speeches shine –
Why, by the verities on thee made good,
May they not be my oracles as well,
10   And set me up in hope? But hush, no more.

> [*Enter* **Macbeth**, *as King*, **Lady Macbeth**, *as Queen*,
> **Lennox, Ross, Lords, Ladies** *and* **Attendants**]

Macbeth   Here's our chief guest.

Lady Macbeth   If he had been forgotten,
It had been as a gap in our great feast,
And all-thing unbecoming.

Macbeth   To-night we hold a solemn supper, sir,
15   And I'll request your presence.

Banquo   Let your highness
Command upon me, to the which my duties
Are with a most indissoluble tie
For ever knit.

Macbeth   Ride you this afternoon?

Act three

Scene 1

At the palace at Forres. **Banquo** *enters, deep in thought.*

Banquo   It's yours now. King, Cawdor, Glamis. Everything, just as the Weird Women promised: and I'm afraid you played a vile game to get it. Yet they said your children wouldn't inherit, but that I myself would be the father of a line of kings. If they speak the truth – as they do in your case, Macbeth – why shouldn't I hope they'll do the same for me? But ssh! [*A trumpet sounds*] I'd better say no more.

[**Macbeth,** *now king, and* **Lady Macbeth,** *now queen, enter, accompanied by* **Lennox, Ross, Lords, Ladies** *and* **Attendants**]

Macbeth   Here's our chief guest!

Lady Macbeth   [*Whispering*] If he had been forgotten, there would have been a very embarrassing gap at our great feast.

Macbeth   [*Taking the hint*] Tonight we are holding a state banquet, sir. I would request your presence.

Banquo   Your Highness may command me. I am forever at your service.

Macbeth   Are you riding this afternoon?

Banquo   Ay, my good lord.

20 **Macbeth**   We should have else desired your good advice
Which still hath been both grave and prosperous
In this day's council; but we'll take to-morrow.
Is't far you ride?

Banquo   As far, my lord, as will fill up the time
25   'Twixt this and supper. Go not my horse the better,
I must become a borrower of the night
For a dark hour or twain.

Macbeth   Fail not our feast.

Banquo   My lord, I will not.

Macbeth   We hear our bloody cousins are bestowed
30   In England and in Ireland, not confessing
Their cruel parricide, filling their hearers
With strange invention: but of that to-morrow,
When therewithal we shall have cause of state
Craving us jointly. Hie you to horse: adieu,
35   Till you return at night. Goes Fleance with you?

Banquo   Ay, my good lord: our time does call upon's.

Macbeth   I wish your horses swift and sure of foot:
And so I do commend you to their backs.
Farewell.

[*Exit* **Banquo**]

40   Let every man be master of his time
Till seven at night; to make society
The sweeter welcome, we will keep ourself
Till supper-time alone: while then, God be with you!

[*All depart but* **Macbeth** *and a* **Servant**]

Sirrah, a word with you: attend those men
45   Our pleasure?

Banquo   Yes, Your Majesty.

Macbeth   Otherwise, we'd have sought your good advice at today's council. It has always been both sound and beneficial. But tomorrow will do. Are you riding far?

Banquo   As far, my lord, as will occupy the time between now and supper. Unless my horse rides fast, I may have to use an hour or two of night.

Macbeth   Don't miss our feast!

Banquo   Your Majesty, I will not.

Macbeth   We hear our murderous cousins are settled in England and Ireland. They won't confess they killed their father. They are telling wild stories to anyone who'll listen. But we can go into that tomorrow when, among other things, we must discuss matters of mutual importance. Off now to your horse. Farewell till you return tonight. Is Fleance going with you?

Banquo   Yes, my good lord. It's time we were off.

Macbeth   May your horses run swift and sure! Here's wishing you a good ride. Farewell!

[**Banquo** *goes*]

Let everyone be free till seven tonight. To make our gathering the more welcome, we'll keep ourselves apart till suppertime. Till then, God be with you!

[*They all go, leaving* **Macbeth** *and a* **Servant**]

You there – I want a word with you. Are those men waiting?

Servant   They are, my lord, without the palace gate.

Macbeth   Bring them before us.

[*The* **Servant** *goes*]

To be thus is nothing,

But to be safely thus: our fears in Banquo
Stick deep, and in his royalty of nature
50   Reigns that which would be feared. 'Tis much he dares,
And, to that dauntless temper of his mind,
He hath a wisdom that doth guide his valour
To act in safety. There is none but he
Whose being I do fear: and under him
55   My Genius is rebuked, as it is said
Mark Antony's was by Caesar. He chid the Sisters,
When first they put the name of king upon me,
And bade them speak to him; then prophet-like
They hailed him father to a line of kings:
60   Upon my head they placed a fruitless crown,
And put a barren sceptre in my gripe,
Thence to be wrenched with an unlineal hand,
No son of mine succeeding. If't be so,
For Banquo's issue have I filed my mind,
65   For them the gracious Duncan have I murdered,
Put rancours in the vessel of my peace
Only for them, and mine eternal jewel
Given to the common enemy of man,
To make them kings, the seed of Banquo kings!
70   Rather than so, come Fate into the list,
And champion me to th'utterance. Who's there?

The **Servant** *enters with two* **Murderers**

Now go to the door, and stay there till we call.

[*Exit* **Servant**]

Servant   They are, my lord. Outside the palace gate.

Macbeth   Bring them to me.

[*The* **Servant** *goes*]

To be thus – a king – is nothing. I must be safely thus. I fear
Banquo deeply. In his regal nature, there's a ruling element to
be feared. He's daring; and with that fearless quality of mind,
he has a wisdom which guides his courage to act in safety. I
fear no one but him. While he's around, I feel constrained: it's
said Mark Antony felt the same way about Caesar. Banquo
scolded the Sisters when they first told me I'd be king, and
ordered them to speak to him. Then, like prophets, they hailed
him as the father of a line of kings. On my head they placed a
sterile crown and put a barren scepter in my hand – to be
wrenched from me by a stranger, instead of handed to a son
of mine. If that is to be so, I've corrupted my mind for
Banquo's offspring. For them, I've murdered the gracious
Duncan. Turned my peace sour merely for them. And
surrendered my immortal soul to the devil – to make them
kings! The sons of Banquo, kings! Rather than that, I
challenge fate to the death! [*He hears a noise*] Who's there?

[*The* **Servant** *enters with two* **Murderers**]

[*To the* **Servant**] Now go to the door and stay there till I call.

[*The* **Servant** *goes*]

Was it not yesterday we spoke together?

1st Murderer   It was, so please your highness.

Macbeth   Well then, now
75   Have you considered of my speeches? Know
That it was he in the times past which held you
So under fortune, which you thought had been
Our innocent self: this I made good to you
In our last conference; passed in probation with you,
80   How you were borne in hand, how crossed, the instruments,
Who wrought with them, and all things else that might
To half a soul and to a notion crazed
Say 'Thus did Banquo'.

1st Murderer   You made it known to us.

Macbeth   I did so; and went further, which is now
85   Our point of second meeting. Do you find
Your patience so predominant in your nature,
That you can let this go? Are you so gospelled,
To pray for this good man, and for his issue,
Whose heavy hand hath bowed you to the grave
90   And beggared yours for ever?

1st Murderer   We are men, my liege.

Macbeth   Ay, in the catalogue ye go for men,
As hounds and greyhounds, mongrels, spaniels, curs,
Shoughs, water-rugs, and demi-wolves, are clept
All by the name of dogs: the valued file
95   Distinguishes the swift, the slow, the subtle,
The housekeeper, the hunter, every one
According to the gift which bounteous nature
Hath in him closed, whereby he does receive
Particular addition, from the bill
100   That writes them all alike: and so of men.
Now, if you have a station in the file,

[*To the* **Murderers**] Wasn't it yesterday we spoke together?

1st Murderer   It was, so please Your Highness.

Macbeth   Well, then. Now have you considered what I said?
You know that it was Banquo, in days gone by, who treated
you badly, when you thought that it had been me. I explained
all this to you at our last conference. I explained to you point
by point how you were misled, how you were thwarted – the
means, the men involved, and everything else that would
prove to even a fool or a madman that "Banquo did this."

1st Murderer   You told us all.

Macbeth   I did indeed. And I went further, which is now the
point of our second meeting. Are you so incredibly patient that
you can forgive all this? So holy that you'll pray for this good
man, and for his children, when his tyranny has bent you to
the grave and beggared your families forever?

1st Murderer   We are men, my liege!

Macbeth   Oh, yes! You might be listed as men, just as hounds,
greyhounds, mongrels, spaniels, strays, shaggy dogs, water
dogs, and shepherd dogs are all called "dogs." But a more
valued list reflects their different qualities; the swift, the slow,
the subtle, the housekeeper, the hunter. Each has a special gift
which nature has given. That's what makes each stand out in
the general classification. It's the same with men. Now, if you
rate yourselves somewhat above the lowest form of life, say

Not i'th' worst rank of manhood, say't,
And I will put that business in your bosoms,
Whose execution takes your enemy off,
105   Grapples you to the heart and love of us
Who wear our health but sickly in his life,
Which in his death were perfect.

2nd Murderer   I am one, my liege.
Whom the vile blows and buffets of the world
Hath so incensed that I am reckless what
110   I do to spite the world.

1st Murderer   And I another
So weary with disasters, tugged with fortune,
That I would set my life on any chance,
To mend it, or be rid on't.

Macbeth   Both of you
Know Banquo was your enemy.

Both Murderers   True, my lord.

115 **Macbeth**   So is he mine: and in such bloody distance,
That every minute of his being thrusts
Against my near'st of life: and though I could
With barefaced power sweep him from my sight,
And bid my will avouch it, yet I must not,
120   For certain friends that are both his and mine,
Whose loves I may not drop, but wail his fall
Who I myself struck down: and thence it is
That I to your assistance do make love,
Masking the business from the common eye,
125   For sundry weighty reasons.

2nd Murderer   We shall, my lord,
Perform what you command us.

1st Murderer   Though our lives –

so. I'll give you a job that – when it's carried out – will remove your enemy and draw you closer to me in regard and affection. My health is undermined while he lives. His death would restore it.

2nd Murderer   I'm the sort of man, my lord, who's been so maddened by life's disasters that I don't care what I do to revenge myself.

1st Murderer   And I'm another. So weary with cruelties, mauled by my misfortune, that to improve my life or be rid of it, I'd wager it on any venture.

Macbeth   Both of you know Banquo was your enemy.

Both Murderers   True, my lord.

Macbeth   He's mine, too. And such a deadly one, that every moment he's alive stabs me to the heart. Of course, I could have him removed quite openly, and say it was my wish. But I mustn't. We have certain mutual friends whose loyalty I need. So I'll have to mourn his death, though I killed him myself. That's why I'm seeking your help. To conceal the truth from the public, for a number of pressing reasons . . .

2nd Murderer   We shall, my lord, do whatever you command us.

1st Murderer   Even though our lives . . .

Macbeth   Your spirits shine through you. Within this hour at
    most
    I will advise you where to plant yourselves,
    Acquaint you with the perfect spy o'th' time,
130   The moment on't, for't must be done to-night,
    And something from the palace; always thought
    That I require a clearness: and with him –
    To leave no rubs nor botches in the work –
    Fleance his son, that keeps him company,
135   Whose absence is no less material to me
    Than is his father's, must embrace the fate
    Of that dark hour. Resolve yourselves apart;
    I'll come to you anon.

Both Murderers   We are resolved, my lord.

Macbeth   I'll call upon you straight; abide within.

                            [*Exeunt* **Murderers**]

    It is concluded: Banquo, thy soul's flight,
    If it find heaven, must find it out to-night.

                                    [*Exit*]

Scene 2

Enter **Lady Macbeth** *and a* **Servant**.

Lady Macbeth   Is Banquo gone from court?

Servant   Ay, madam, but returns again to-night.

Lady Macbeth   Say to the king, I would attend his leisure
    For a few words.

Macbeth   [*Interrupting in his excitement*] That's the spirit! Within the hour, I'll tell you where to hide yourselves, and what's the best time for it. It must be done tonight, away from the palace. Remember – I can't be involved. And also, to make a clean job of it, I want his son Fleance, who'll be with him, to share the same fate. His removal is just as important to me. Go and talk it over. I'll join you soon.

Both Murderers   We've made up our minds, my lord.

Macbeth   I'll be with you right away. Stay in my antechamber.

[*They leave*]

That's that. Banquo, if your soul is bound for heaven, it will reach there tonight!

[*He goes*]

Scene 2

Lady Macbeth, *looking weary, enters with a* **Servant**.

Lady Macbeth   Has Banquo left court?

Servant   Yes, madam, but he'll be back again tonight.

Lady Macbeth   Tell the king I'd like a few words with him.

Servant	Madam, I will.

[*He goes*]

Lady Macbeth   Nought's had, all's spent,
5   Where our desire is got without content:
       'Tis safer to be that which we destroy
       Than by destruction dwell in doubtful joy.

[*Enter* **Macbeth**]

       How now, my lord! why do you keep alone,
       Of sorriest fancies your companions making,
10   Using those thoughts which should indeed have died
       With them they think on? Things without all remedy
       Should be without regard: what's done, is done.

Macbeth   We have scotched the snake, not killed it:
       She'll close and be herself, whilst our poor malice
15   Remains in danger of her former tooth.
       But let the frame of things disjoint, both the worlds suffer,
       Ere we will eat our meal in fear and sleep
       In the affliction of these terrible dreams
       That shake us nightly: better be with the dead,
20   Whom we, to gain our peace, have sent to peace,
       Than on the torture of the mind to lie
       In restless ecstasy. Duncan is in his grave;
       After life's fitful fever he sleeps well;
       Treason has done his worst: nor steel, nor poison,
25   Malice domestic, foreign levy, nothing,
       Can touch him further.

Lady Macbeth   Come on;
       Gentle my lord, sleek o'er your rugged looks,
       Be bright and jovial among your guests to-night.

Servant   Madam, I will.

[*He goes*]

Lady Macbeth   Nothing's gained, all's lost, when a wish fulfilled brings no contentment. It's better to be the victim than to live in worry on the proceeds of the crime.

[**Macbeth** *enters*]

Well, now, my lord! Why do you stay by yourself, with morbid thoughts as your only companions, thoughts that should have died with the people they brood on? What can't be cured has to be endured. What's done is done.

Macbeth   We've wounded the snake, not killed it. It'll heal and be a snake again, while we remain in danger of its bite. The universe can split; heaven and earth can fall apart. But we won't eat our meals in fear or keep suffering nightmares in our sleep! Better to be with the dead – whom we, to gain our peace, have sent to their eternal peace – than to be tortured with mental agony! Duncan is in his grave. After the ups and downs of life, he sleeps soundly. Treason has done its worst. Neither sword, nor poison, nor rebellions at home, nor threatening invasion forces can touch him now.

Lady Macbeth   Come on, dear husband. Don't look so careworn. Be bright and cheerful among your guests tonight.

Macbeth   So shall I, love, and so I pray be you:
30   Let your remembrance apply to Banquo;
Present him eminence, both with eye and tongue:
Unsafe the while, that we
Must lave our honours in these flattering streams,
And make our faces vizards to our hearts,
35   Disguising what they are.

Lady Macbeth   You must leave this.

Macbeth   O, full of scorpions is my mind, dear wife!
Thou know'st that Banquo and his Fleance lives.

Lady Macbeth   But in them nature's copy's not eterne.

Macbeth   There's comfort yet; they are assailable,
40   Then be thou jocund: ere the bat hath flown
His cloistered flight, ere to black Hecate's summons
The shard-borne beetle with his drowsy hums
Hath rung night's yawning peal, there shall be done
A deed of dreadful note.

Lady Macbeth   What's to be done?

45 **Macbeth**   Be innocent of the knowledge, dearest chuck,
Till thou applaud the deed. Come, seeling night,
Scarf up the tender eye of pitiful day,
And with thy bloody and invisible hand
Cancel and tear to pieces that great bond
50   Which keeps me paled! Light thickens, and the crow
Makes wing to th' rooky wood:
Good things of day begin to droop and drowse,
Whiles night's black agents to their preys do rouse.
Thou marvell'st at my words: but hold thee still;
55   Things bad begun make strong themselves by ill:
So, prithee, go with me.

[Exeunt]

Macbeth   So I shall, love. And so I hope will you. Pay special attention to Banquo. Shower him with looks and words. This is an unsafe time when we must hide our faces behind flattering masks, disguising what's in our hearts.

Lady Macbeth   You must stop this.

Macbeth   Oh, my mind is full of scorpions, dear wife! You know that Banquo and his Fleance live!

Lady Macbeth   They're not immortal.

Macbeth   That's a comfort. They can be dealt with. So cheer up. Before the bat goes hunting, before the sound of beetles fills night's air, there shall be done a deed of dreadful importance!

Lady Macbeth   What's to be done?

Macbeth   Stay in ignorance, dearest chick, till you praise the deed. Come, blinding night! Cover the tender eye of pitying day; and with your bloody and invisible hand, destroy the life that keeps me in fear. Night falls. The crow flies homeward to the gloomy wood. The good things of day begin to droop and become drowsy while the predators of the dark stir about their tasks. My words amaze you. But hold on: "Bad deeds grow strong through wickedness." So please, go with me.

[*They go*]

Scene 3

Some way from the palace. Enter three **Murderers**.

1st Murderer   But who did bid thee join with us?

3rd Murderer   Macbeth.

2nd Murderer   He needs not our mistrust, since he delivers
Our offices and what we have to do,
To the direction just.

1st Murderer   Then stand with us.
5   The west yet glimmers with some streaks of day:
Now spurs the lated traveller apace
To gain the timely inn, and near approaches
The subject of our watch.

3rd Murderer   Hark! I hear horses.

Banquo   Give us a light there, ho!

2nd Murderer   Then 'tis he; the rest
10   That are within the note of expectation
Already are i'th' court.

1st Murderer   His horses go about.

3rd Murderer   Almost a mile: but he does usually –
So all men do – from hence to th' palace gate
Make it their walk.

[*Enter* **Banquo** *and* **Fleance** *with a torch*]

15 **2nd Murderer**   A light, a light!

3rd Murderer   'Tis he.

1st Murderer   Stand to't.

Scene 3

*Some distance from the palace. Three **Murderers** stand waiting.*

1st Murderer   Who told you to join us?

3rd Murderer   Macbeth.

2nd Murderer   He's no cause to distrust us. He told us our duties and gave us exact orders.

1st Murderer   Join us then. There are still some streaks of daylight in the west. Now's the time late travelers spur their horses, hoping to reach a convenient inn. And the man we are waiting for is getting nearer.

3rd Murderer   Listen – I hear horses.

Banquo   [*Offstage*] Give me a light there, will you!

2nd Murderer   That's he. The other guests are already at the court.

1st Murderer   He's left the horses.

3rd Murderer   Almost a mile. But he usually does. Everyone does. They walk from here to the palace gate.

   [**Banquo** *and* **Fleance** *enter, carrying torches*]

2nd Murderer   A light, a light!

3rd Murderer   That's he!

1st Murderer   Get ready!

Banquo   It will be rain tonight.

1st Murderer   Let it come down.

[*They set upon* **Banquo**]

Banquo   O, treachery! Fly, good Fleance, fly, fly, fly!
   Thou mayst revenge. O slave!

[*He dies;* **Fleance** *escapes*]

20 **3rd Murderer**   Who did strike out the light?

1st Murderer   Was't not the way?

3rd Murderer   There's but one down; the son is fled.

2nd Murderer   We have lost
   Best half of our affair.

1st Murderer   Well, let's away, and say how much is done.

[*Exeunt*]

Scene 4

The hall of the palace. A banquet prepared. Enter **Macbeth, Lady Macbeth, Ross, Lennox, Lords** *and* **Attendants**.

Macbeth   You know your own degrees, sit down: at first
   And last the hearty welcome.

Lords   Thanks to your majesty.

Banquo   [*Pleasantly*] It's going to rain tonight.

1st Murderer   Let it pour!

[*The first* **Murderer** *strikes out the torch while the others stab* **Banquo**]

Banquo   Treachery! Run, Fleance, run! run! run! You can revenge me. Oh, villains . . .

[*He is killed.* **Fleance** *escapes*]

3rd Murderer   Who put out the light?

1st Murderer   Wasn't that the plan?

3rd Murderer   We've only killed one. The son escaped.

2nd Murderer   We've failed in the best half of our job.

1st Murderer   Well, let's go and report how much we've done.

[*They go*]

Scene 4

The hall of the palace. A banquet has been prepared. **Macbeth, Lady Macbeth, Ross, Lennox, Lords** *and* **Attendants** *enter.*

Macbeth   You know your ranks. Sit down accordingly. From the top table downward, I give you hearty welcome!

Lords   Thanks to Your Majesty!

Macbeth   Ourself will mingle with society,
5   And play the humble host:
Our hostess keeps her state, but in best time
We will require her welcome.

Lady Macbeth   Pronounce it for me, sir, to all our friends,
For my heart speaks they are welcome.

[*The* **First Murderer** *appears at the door*]

10 **Macbeth**   See, they encounter thee with their hearts' thanks.
Both sides are even: here I'll sit i'th' midst:
Be large in mirth, anon we'll drink a measure
The table round. [*To* **Murderer**] There's blood upon thy face.

1st Murderer   'Tis Banquo's then.

15 **Macbeth**   'Tis better thee without than he within.
Is he dispatched?

1st Murderer   My lord, his throat is cut; that I did for him.

Macbeth   Thou art the best o'th' cut-throats. Yet he's good
That did the like for Fleance: if thou didst it,
20   Thou art the nonpareil.

1st Murderer   Most royal sir,
Fleance is 'scaped.

Macbeth   Then comes my fit again: I had else been perfect;
Whole as the marble, founded as the rock,
As broad and general as the casing air:
25   But now I am cabined, cribbed, confined, bound in
To saucy doubts and fears. But Banquo's safe?

1st Murderer   Ay, my good lord: safe in a ditch he bides,
With twenty trenched gashes on his head;
The least a death to nature.

Macbeth   I'll mingle with the guests and play the humble host. Our hostess will stay seated. She'll welcome you at the proper time.

Lady Macbeth   Do so on my behalf, sir, to all our friends, for they are welcome with all my heart.

[*The* **Lords** *rise and bow. The* **First Murderer** *enters*]

Macbeth   [*To* **Lady Macbeth**] See – their heartfelt thanks are yours. [*He looks for a vacant seat*] Both sides are even. I'll sit here in the middle. [*He spots the* **Murderer**] Enjoy yourselves! We'll pass around the drinking cup just now!

[*To the* **Murderer**] There's blood on your face.

1st Murderer   It's Banquo's then.

Macbeth   It's better outside you than inside him. Is he killed?

1st Murderer   My lord, his throat is cut. That I did for him.

Macbeth   You are the best of cutthroats! Yet he's as good who did the same for Fleance. If you did it, you have no equal!

1st Murderer   Most royal sir – Fleance escaped.

Macbeth   My illness comes back. I'd otherwise be sound. Flawless as marble. Solid as rock. As free and liberated as the air around us. Now I'm closed in, cramped, confined – the prisoner of nagging doubts and fears. But Banquo's fixed?

1st Murderer   Yes, my good lord. Safe in a ditch he dwells, with twenty trench-like gashes in his head, the least of them fatal.

Macbeth   Thanks for that:
30   There the grown serpent lies; the worm that's fled
Hath nature that in time will venom breed,
No teeth for th' present. Get thee gone; to-morrow
We'll hear ourselves again.

[*Exit* **Murderer**]

Lady Macbeth   My royal lord,
You do not give the cheer. The feast is sold
35   That is not often vouched, while 'tis a-making,
'Tis given with welcome: to feed were best at home;
From thence the sauce to meat is ceremony;
Meeting were bare without it.

[*The ghost of* **Banquo** *enters and sits in Macbeth's place.*]

Macbeth   Sweet remembrancer!
Now good digestion wait on appetite,
40   And health on both!

Lennox   May't please your highness sit?

Macbeth   Here had we now our country's honour roofed,
Were the graced person of our Banquo present;
Who may I rather challenge for unkindness
Than pity for mischance!

Ross   His absence, sir,
45   Lays blame upon his promise. Please't your highness
To grace us with your royal company?

Macbeth   The table's full.

Lennox   Here is a place reserved, sir.

Macbeth   Where?

Macbeth   Thanks for that. The adult serpent's dead. The
youngster that escaped has the makings of trouble, but he's
harmless now. Go. Tomorrow we'll talk together again.

[*The* **First Murderer** *leaves*]

Lady Macbeth   My royal lord, you do not play the host! A
tavern meal lacks welcoming toasts. Mere food alone is best
consumed at home. What gives a feast its flavor is the
ceremony. It's a poor feast without it.

[*The ghost of* **Banquo** *enters and sits in* **Macbeth**'s *place*]

Macbeth   [*Affectionately*] I'm glad you reminded me! [*To the
company*] To appetites and good digestion! And health to
both!

Lennox   Do please sit, sir.

Macbeth   We'd have here under one roof the noblest in the
land if our friend Banquo were present. I hope it's a case of
thoughtlessness, not mischance.

Ross   His absence, sir, is a breach of his promise. [*Indicating
a seat*] Would Your Highness grace us with your royal
company?

Macbeth   The table's full.

Lennox   Here's a place reserved, sir.

Macbeth   Where?

Lennox   Here, my good lord. What is't that moves your
    highness?

50 **Macbeth**   Which of you have done this?

Lords   What, my good lord?

Macbeth   Thou canst not say I did it: never shake
    Thy gory locks at me.

Ross   Gentlemen, rise, his highness is not well.

Lady Macbeth   Sit, worthy friends: my lord is often thus,
55   And hath been from his youth: pray you, keep seat,
    The fit is momentary; upon a thought
    He will again be well: if much you note him,
    You shall offend him and extend his passion:
    Feed, and regard him not. Are you a man?

60 **Macbeth**   Ay, and a bold one, that dare look on that
    Which might appal the devil.

Lady Macbeth   O proper stuff!
    This is the very painting of your fear:
    This is the air-drawn dagger which, you said,
    Led you to Duncan. O, these flaws and starts
65   Impostors to true fear would well become
    A woman's story at a winter's fire,
    Authorized by her grandam. Shame itself!
    Why do you make such faces? When all's done,
    You look but on a stool.

70 **Macbeth**   Prithee, see there! behold! look! lo! how say you?
    Why, what care I? If thou canst nod, speak too.
    If charnel-houses and our graves must send
    Those that we bury back, our monuments
    Shall be the maws of kites.

                                        [*The* **Ghost** *vanishes*]

Lennox   Here, my good lord. What is upsetting Your Highness?

Macbeth   [*Pointing to the* **Ghost**] Which of you has done this?

Lords   What, my good lord? [*The* **Ghost** *makes signals*]

Macbeth   You cannot say I did it! Don't shake your gory locks at me!

Ross   Gentlemen, rise. His Highness is not well.

Lady Macbeth   Sit, good friends. My lord is often like this and has been since his youth. Please, stay in your seats. The fit will soon pass. He'll be well again in a moment. If you take too much notice, you'll offend him and extend his fit. Eat up, and ignore him. [*To* **Macbeth**, *angrily*] Are you a man?

Macbeth   Yes, and a bold one, that dares to look at what might scare the devil.

Lady Macbeth   Oh, really! This is a fear of your imagination. This is that airborne dagger which you said led you to Duncan! Oh, these fits and starts – these fake fears – would better suit an old wife's tale told at a winter fireside. Shame on you! Why are you making such faces? When all is said and done, you are only looking at a stool!

Macbeth   See there – look! There! Now what do you say? [*To the* **Ghost**] Why, what do I care? If you can nod, speak too! If graves and tombs will send back those we bury, we'd better feed our corpses to the vultures!

[*The* **Ghost** *disappears*]

75 **Lady Macbeth**   What! quite unmanned in folly?

Macbeth   If I stand here, I saw him.

Lady Macbeth   Fie, for shame!

Macbeth   Bood hath been shed ere now, i'th'olden time,
Ere humane statute purged the gentle weal;
Ay, and since too, murders have been performed
Too terrible for the ear: the time has been,
80 That, when the brains were out, the man would die,
And there an end: but now they rise again,
With twenty mortal murders on their crowns,
And push us from our stools. This is more strange
Than such a murder is.

Lady Macbeth   My worthy lord,
85 Your noble friends do lack you.

Macbeth   I do forget.
Do not muse at me, my most worthy friends;
I have a strange infirmity, which is nothing
To those that know me. Come, love and health to all;
Then I'll sit down. Give me some wine, fill full.

[*The* **Ghost** *returns*]

90 I drink to th' general joy o'th' whole table,
And to our dear friend Banquo, whom we miss;
Would he were here! to all, and him we thirst,
And all to all!

Lords   Our duties, and the pledge.

95 **Macbeth**   Avaunt! and quit my sight! let the earth hide thee!
Thy bones are marrowless, thy blood is cold;
Thou hast no speculation in those eyes
Which thou dost glare with!

Lady Macbeth   Is your foolishness taking away your manhood?

Macbeth   As sure as I stand here, I saw him!

Lady Macbeth   What nonsense!

Macbeth   [*To himself*] Blood has been shed before now, in the old days before just laws reformed society. Yes, and since then, too, murders have been committed, too terrible to hear about. There was a time when smashed brains meant the man would die, and that was that. But now men rise again, with twenty fatal gashes in their heads, and steal our seats. This is stranger than murder.

Lady Macbeth   My worthy lord. Your noble friends are missing you.

Macbeth   [*Recovering*] I'm forgetting. [*To the guests*] Don't brood over me, my most worthy friends. I have a strange disability, which is nothing to those who know me. Come! [*Raising his glass*] Love and health to all! Then I'll sit down. Give me some wine. Fill it up!

[*The **Ghost** returns*]

I drink to the general joy of the whole table, and to our dear friend Banquo, who is not present. Would he were here! [*Proposing a toast*] To all, and to him we lack, and health to everyone!

Lords   Our duties, and the toast!

Macbeth   [*Seeing the **Ghost***]Go away! Quit my sight! Back to your grave! Your bones are marrowless, your blood is cold. You have no power of seeing in those glaring eyes!

Lady Macbeth   Think of this, good peers,
But as a thing of custom: 'tis no other;
100   Only it spoils the pleasure of the time.

Macbeth   What man dare, I dare:
Approach thou like the rugged Russian bear,
The armed rhinoceros, or th'Hyrcan tiger,
Take any shape but that, and my firm nerves
105   Shall never tremble: or be alive again,
And dare me to the desert with thy sword;
If trembling I inhabit then, protest me
The baby of a girl. Hence, horrible shadow!
Unreal mock'ry, hence!

[*The* **Ghost** *goes*]

                              Why, so; being gone,
110   I am a man again. Pray you, sit still.

Lady Macbeth   You have displaced the mirth, broke the good
    meeting,
With most admired disorder.

Macbeth   Can such things be,
And overcome us like a summer's cloud,
Without our special wonder? You make me strange
115   Even to the disposition that I owe,
When now I think you can behold such sights,
And keep the natural ruby of your cheeks,
When mine is blanched with fear.

Ross   What sights, my lord?

Lady Macbeth   I pray you, speak not; he grows worse and
    worse;
Question enrages him: at once, good night.
120   Stand not upon the order of your going,
But go at once.

Lady Macbeth   Think of this, good noblemen, as a chronic ailment. That's what it is. Unfortunately, it upsets things.

Macbeth   [*To the* **Ghost**] Whatever man dares, I dare! Approach me like a rugged Russian bear, an armor-plated rhinoceros, or a wild tiger! Take any shape but your own, and my firm nerves will never tremble. Or come alive again, and dare me to the desert with your sword! If I fall to trembling then, call me a baby girl! Begone, horrible shadow! Unreal mockery, begone!

[*The* **Ghost** *goes*]

Why, then. Once it is gone, I am a man again. [*To the guests*] Please – keep your seats.

Lady Macbeth   [*Reproaching him*] You've spoiled the enjoyment – destroyed the atmosphere – with your ridiculous behavior!

Macbeth   Can such things happen – like a cloud spoiling a summer's day – without astonishing us? You make me doubt myself. You can behold such sights and keep the natural color of your cheeks. Mine turn white with fear.

Ross   What sights, my lord?

Lady Macbeth   Please don't say anything. He gets worse and worse. Questions enrage him. Now, goodnight! No ceremonial leave-taking. Go at once.

Lennox   Good night, and better health
Attend his majesty!

Lady Macbeth   A kind good night to all!

[They leave]

Macbeth It will have blood; they say, blood will have blood:
125   Stones have been known to move and trees to speak;
Augures and understood relations have
By magot-pies and choughs and rooks brought forth
The secret'st man of blood. What is the night?

Lady Macbeth   Almost at odds with morning, which is which.

130 **Macbeth**   How say'st thou, that Macduff denies his person
At our great bidding?

Lady Macbeth   Did you send to him, sir?

Macbeth   I hear it by the way; but I will send:
There's not a one of them but in his house
I keep a servant fee'd. I will to-morrow,
135   And betimes I will, to the Weird Sisters:
More shall they speak; for now I am bent to know,
By the worst means, the worst. For mine own good
All causes shall give way: I am in blood
Stepped in so far that, should I wade no more,
140   Returning were as tedious as go o'er:
Strange things I have in head that will to hand,
Which must be acted ere they may be scanned.

Lady Macbeth   You lack the season of all natures, sleep.

Macbeth   Come, we'll to sleep. My strange and self-abuse
145   Is the initiate fear that wants hard use:
We are yet but young in deed.

[Exeunt]

Lennox   Good night, and may His Majesty enjoy better health.

Lady Macbeth   A kind goodnight to all!

[*She hustles them out*]

Macbeth   It will have blood. They say, "Blood will have blood." Gravestones have been known to move, and trees to speak. Magpies, crows and ravens have spotted the most secretive of murderers. What time of night is it?

Lady Macbeth   Almost morning. It's hard to tell the difference.

Macbeth   What do you make of Macduff ignoring our invitation?

Lady Macbeth   Did you summon him, sir?

Macbeth   I hear rumors. But I'll summon him all right. I keep a spy in all their houses. Early tomorrow, I'll go to the Weird Sisters. They must tell me more. I must know the worst, by whatever means. Nothing shall stand in the way of my interests. My path has been so bloody, stopping now and going back would be no easier than going forward. I have some projects in my head that need action first and thought later. They must be done before they are thought of.

Lady Macbeth   You lack what all creatures need – sleep.

Macbeth   Come, we'll go to sleep. My delusions are beginner's fear. I need experience. We've only just started.

[*They go*]

Scene 5

A heath. Thunder. Enter the three **Witches,** *meeting* **Hecate.**

1st Witch   Why, how now, Hecate, you look angerly.

Hecate   Have I not reason, beldams as you are,
Saucy and overbold? How did you dare
To trade and traffic with Macbeth
5 In riddles and affairs of death;
And I, the mistress of your charms,
The close contriver of all harms,
Was never called to bear my part,
Or show the glory of our art?
10 And, which is worse, all you have done
Hath been but for a wayward son,
Spiteful and wrathful, who (as others do)
Loves for his own ends, not for you.
But make amends now: get you gone,
15 And at the pit of Acheron
Meet me i'th' morning: thither he
Will come to know his destiny.
Your vessels and your spells provide,
Your charms and everything beside.
20 I am for th'air; this night I'll spend
Unto a dismal and a fatal end.
Great business must be wrought ere noon:
Upon the corner of the moon
There hangs a vap'rous drop profound:
25 I'll catch it ere it come to ground:
And that distilled by magic sleights
Shall raise such artificial sprites
As by the strength of their illusion
Shall draw him on to his confusion.
30 He shall spurn fate, scorn death, and bear

Scene 5

On the heath. It is thundering. The three **Witches** *enter, meeting* **Hecate,** *their queen.*

1st Witch Greetings, Hecate! You look angry!

Hecate Haven't I reason, you saucy old hag?
How did you dare to let your tongue wag,
To trade and traffic with Macbeth,
In riddles and affairs of death?
And I, the leader of your covey
Could play no part, nor share the glory?
And what is worse, all you have done
Has been to aid a wayward son
All spite and wrath, and selfish too –
Loves but himself and none of you!
Now make amends. Bid farewell
And meet me at the gates of Hell
Tomorrow morn. He'll thither go
His future destiny to know.
Your cauldrons and your spells provide:
Your charms, and everything beside.
I'll disappear. Tonight I'll spend
Watching a mortal's fatal end.
Great business must be done ere noon.
Now, on the corner of the moon
There hangs a vaporous drop profound
I'll catch before it comes to ground.
And that, distilled by magic sleights,
Will raise such artificial sprites
As by the strength of their illusion
He'll be drawn to his confusion.
He'll spurn his fate, scorn death, and bear

His hopes 'bove wisdom, grace, and fear:
And you all know security
Is mortals' chiefest enemy.

Music and a song: 'Come away, come away,'

Hark, I am called: my little spirit, see,
35 Sits in a foggy cloud, and stays for me.

[*She flies away*]

1st Witch   Come, let's make haste; she'll soon be back again.

[*They vanish*]

Scene 6

Forres. The Palace. Enter **Lennox** *and another* **Lord**.

Lennox   My former speeches have but hit your thoughts,
Which can interpret farther: only I say
Things have been strangely borne. The gracious Duncan
Was pitied of Macbeth: marry he was dead:
5 And the right valiant Banquo walked too late –
Whom you may say if't please you Fleance killed,
For Fleance fled: men must not walk too late.
Who cannot want the thought, how monstrous
It was for Malcolm and for Donalbain
10 To kill their gracious father? damned fact!
How it did grieve Macbeth! did he not straight,
In pious rage, the two delinquents tear,
That were the slaves of drink and thralls of sleep?

His hopes above wisdom, grace and fear.
As you all know, man's chiefest enemy
Is overconfidence and complacency.

[*Sounds of music, and a song "Come away, come away"*]

Listen! I'm called. My little spirit, see,
Sits in a foggy cloud waiting for me.

[*She flies away*]

1st Witch   Come, let's hurry. She'll be back again soon.

[*They disappear*]

Scene 6

The palace at Forres. **Lennox** *and another* **Lord** *enter.*

Lennox   [*Speaking with mounting sarcasm*] What I've been
saying ties in with your own thinking, so you can draw your
own conclusions. I say only this: things have happened very
strangely. The gracious Duncan was pitied by Macbeth. Then
he was dead. And the valiant Banquo walked too late at night.
You can say, if it suits you, that Fleance killed him, because
Fleance fled. Men really should not walk out late! Who hasn't
thought how monstrous it was for Malcolm and for Donalbain
to kill their father? That damnable act! How it grieved
Macbeth! Didn't he immediately, in pious rage, stab the two
thugs who were helpless with drink and fast asleep? Wasn't

Was not that nobly done? Ay, and wisely too;
15   For 'twould have angered any heart alive
To hear the men deny't. So that, I say,
He has borne all things well: and I do think
That, had he Duncan's sons under his key –
As, an't please heaven, he shall not – they should find
20   What 'twere to kill a father, so should Fleance.
But, peace! for from broad words, and 'cause he failed
His presence at the tyrant's feast, I hear,
Macduff lives in disgrace. Sir, can you tell
Where he bestows himself?

Lord   The son of Duncan
25   From whom this tyrant holds the due of birth
Lives in the English court, and is received
Of the most pious Edward with such grace
That the malevolence of fortune nothing
Takes from his high respect. Thither Macduff
30   Is gone to pray the holy king, upon his aid
To wake Northumberland and warlike Siward,
That by the help of these – with Him above
To ratify the work – we may again
Give to our tables meat, sleep to our nights;
35   Free from our feasts and banquets bloody knives;
Do faithful homage and receive free honours;
All which we pine for now. And this report
Hath so exasperate the king that he
Prepares for some attempt of war.

Lennox   Sent he to Macduff?

40   **Lord**   He did: and with an absolute 'Sir, not I',
The cloudy messenger turns me his back,
And hums, as who should say, 'You'll rue the time
That clogs me with this answer.'

that nobly done? Yes, and wisely too. It would have angered anyone with a heart to hear the men deny the deed. So I say he has acted properly. And I think if he had Duncan's sons in his dungeons – which, with God's mercy, he never will – they'd soon find out what happens to those who kill a father. So should Fleance. But enough. Because of things he's said, and for missing the tyrant's feast, I hear Macduff is in disgrace. Do you know where he has gone?

Lord   Duncan's son, whose throne the tyrant has usurped, lives in the English court. He is treated by the holy king, Edward the Confessor, with such graciousness that his ill-fortune in no way diminishes his high rank. Macduff has gone there to beg the holy king to come to his aid, by rousing warlike Siward and his men of Northumberland. With their help, and God behind them, we may again entertain our guests, sleep at night, banish bloody knives from our feasts and banquets, pay loyal homage and receive impartial honors – all of which we pine for now. And this report has so angered Macbeth that he prepares for war.

Lennox   Did he summon Macduff?

Lord   He did. And he replied with a curt "Sir, not I." The angry messenger turned his back and hummed, as if to say, "You'll regret the time you gave me that sort of answer to deliver."

Lennox   And that well might
Advise him to a caution, to hold what distance
45   His wisdom can provide. Some holy angel
Fly to the court of England and unfold
His message ere he come, that a swift blessing
May soon return to this our suffering country
Under a hand accursed!

Lord   I'll send my prayers with him.

[Exeunt]

Lennox   And that ought to warn him to keep his distance. May some holy angel fly to the court of England ahead of him, to speed the day of liberation for our suffering country!

Lord   I'll send my prayers with him.

   [*They go*]

Act four

Scene 1

A cavern and in the middle a fiery cauldron. Thunder. Enter the three **Witches**.

1st Witch   Thrice the brinded cat hath mewed.

2nd Witch   Thrice and once the hedge-pig whined.

3rd Witch   Harpier cries: 'Tis time, 'tis time.

1st Witch   Round about the cauldron go:
5   In the poisoned entrails throw.
Toad, that under cold stone
Days and nights has thirty-one
Sweltered venom sleeping got,
Boil thou first i'th' charmed pot!

10 **All**   Double, double toil and trouble;
Fire burn and cauldron bubble.

2nd Witch   Fillet of a fenny snake,
In the cauldron boil and bake:
Eye of newt and toe of frog,
15   Wool of bat and tongue of dog,
Adder's fork and blind-worm's sting,
Lizard's leg and howlet's wing,
For a charm of powerful trouble,
Like a hell-broth boil and bubble.

20 **All**   Double, double toil and trouble:
Fire burn and cauldron bubble.

3rd Witch   Scale of dragon, tooth of wolf,
Witch's mummy, maw and gulf

Act four

Scene 1

A cavern. In the middle, a boiling cauldron. Thunder and lightning. The three **Witches** *enter.*

1st Witch Thrice the tabby cat has mewed.

2nd Witch Thrice plus once the hedgehog whined.

3rd Witch The fiend cries "It's time, it's time!"

1st Witch Round about the cauldron go:
In the poisoned entrails throw.
Toad that sweltered under stone
For days and nights has poisoned grown.
A month of venom it has got,
So boil them first in the charmed pot!

All Double, double, toil and trouble,
Fire burn and cauldron bubble.

2nd Witch Fillet of a marshland snake,
In the cauldron boil and bake;
Eye of newt and toe of frog,
Wool of bat and tongue of dog,
Adder's fork and blindworm's sting,
Lizard's leg and young owl's wing,
For a charm of powerful trouble,
Like a hell-broth, boil and bubble.

All Double, double, toil and trouble,
Fire burn and cauldron bubble.

3rd Witch Scale of dragon, wolf's tooth pullèd,
Witch's mummy, guts and gullet

Of the ravined salt-sea shark,
25 Root of hemlock digged i'th' dark,
Liver of blaspheming Jew,
Gall of goat and slips of yew
Slivered in the moon's eclipse,
Nose of Turk and Tartar's lips,
30 Finger of birth-strangled babe
Ditch-delivered by a drab,
Make the gruel thick and slab:
Add thereto a tiger's chaudron,
For th'ingredience of our cauldron.

35 **All**   Double, double toil and trouble;
Fire burn and cauldron bubble.

2nd Witch   Cool it with a baboon's blood,
Then the charm is firm and good.

[*Enter* **Hecate**]

Hecate   O, well done! I commend your pains,
40 And every one shall shall i'th' gains:
And now about the cauldron sing,
Like elves and fairies in a ring,
Enchanting all that you put in.

Music and a song: Black spirits. **Hecate** *goes*

2nd Witch   By the pricking of my thumbs,
45 Something wicked this way comes:
Open, locks,
Whoever knocks!

[*Enter* **Macbeth**]

Macbeth   How now, you secret, black, and midnight hags!
What is't you do?

Of the captured salt-sea shark,
Root of hemlock, dug in the dark,
Liver of blaspheming Jew,
Gall of goat and slips of yew
Splintered in the moon's eclipse,
Nose of Turk and Tartar's lips,
Finger of a strangled brat
Ditch-delivered by a slut:
Add tiger entrails, steaming hot,
To thicken all that's in our pot.

All   Double, double, toil and trouble,
Fire burn and cauldron bubble.

2nd Witch   Cool it with a baboon's blood,
Then the charm is firm and good.

[**Hecate** *joins the other three* **Witches**]

Hecate   Oh, well done! I admire your pains
And everyone shall share the gains.
And now about the cauldron sing,
Like elves and fairies in a ring,
Enchanting all that you put in.

[*There is music, and a song "Black Spirits."* **Hecate** *leaves*]

2nd Witch   By the pricking of my thumbs,
Something wicked this way comes;
Open, locks – whoever knocks!

[**Macbeth** *enters*]

Macbeth   Well, you secret, black, and midnight hags! What are
you up to now?

All   A deed without a name.

50 **Macbeth**   I conjure you, by that which you profess
          Howe'er you come to know it answer me:
          Though you untie the winds and let them fight
          Against the churches; though the yesty waves
          Confound and swallow navigation up;
55   Though bladed corn be lodged and trees blown down;
          Though castles topple on their warders' heads;
          Though palaces and pyramids do slope
          Their heads to their foundations; though the treasure
          Of Nature's germens tumble all together,
60   Even till destruction sicken; answer me
          To what I ask you.

     1st Witch   Speak.

     2nd Witch   Demand.

     3rd Witch   We'll answer.

     1st Witch   Say if th'hadst rather hear it from our mouths,
          Or from our masters.

     Macbeth   Call 'em, let me see 'em!

     1st Witch   Pour in sow's blood, that hath eaten
65   Her nine farrow; grease that's sweaten
          From the murderer's gibbet throw
          Into the flame.

     All   Come, high or low;
          Thyself and office deftly show.

     [*Thunder*. **First Apparition:** *an armed head*]

     Macbeth   Tell me, thou unknown power –

     1st Witch   He knows thy thought:
70   Hear his speech, but say thou nought.

All   A deed without a name.

Macbeth   I call upon you, in the name of your art – whatever be the source of your knowledge – to answer me! Though you untie winds that batter churches; though stormy waves destroy and swallow up shipping; though ripe corn is flattened, trees are blown down, and castles are toppled on their watchmen's heads; though palaces and pyramids lean toward their foundations; though atoms mix in chaos, and destruction sickens itself – answer me when I ask!

1st Witch   Speak.

2nd Witch   Demand.

3rd Witch   We'll answer.

1st Witch   Say if you'd rather hear it from our mouths or from our masters'?

Macbeth   Call them. Let me see them.

1st Witch   Pour in sow's blood that has eaten
Her nine piglets; throw into the flame
Grease that's sweat from a gallows frame!

All   Come, high in hell, or low –
Yourself and your description show!

[*A clap of thunder. The* **First Apparition** *is a head, wearing armor*]

Macbeth   Tell me, you unknown power –

1st Witch   He knows your thoughts. Hear his speech, but speak not.

1st Apparition   Macbeth! Macbeth! Macbeth! beware
  Macduff,
Beware the thane of Fife. Dismiss me. Enough.

[*Descends*]

Macbeth   Whate'er thou art, for thy good caution thanks;
Thou hast harped my fear aright. But one word more –

75 **1st Witch**   He will not be commanded: here's another,
More potent than the first.

Thunder. **Second Apparition:** *a bloody child*

2nd Apparition   Macbeth! Macbeth! Macbeth!

Macbeth   Had I three ears, I'd hear thee.

2nd Apparition   Be bloody, bold, and resolute: laugh to scorn
80 The power of man; for none of woman born
Shall harm Macbeth.

[*Descends*]

Macbeth   Then live, Macduff: what need I fear of thee?
But yet I'll make assurance double sure,
And take a bond of fate: thou shalt not live,
85 That I may tell pale-hearted fear it lies,
And sleep in spite of thunder.

[*Thunder*. **Third Apparition:** *a child crowned, with a tree in his
hand*]

                              What is this,
That rises like the issue of a king,
And wears upon his baby-brow the round
And top of sovereignty?

1st Apparition   Macbeth! Macbeth! Macbeth! Beware Macduff! Beware the thane of Fife! Dismiss me. Enough.

[*The* **Apparition** *goes*]

Macbeth   Whatever you are, thanks for your warning! You've rightly guessed my fear. One word more –

1st Witch   He will not be ordered. Here's another, more powerful than the first.

[*Thunder. A* **Second Apparition** *appears – a blood-covered child.*]

2nd Apparition   Macbeth! Macbeth! Macbeth!

Macbeth   Had I three ears, I'd hear you!

2nd Apparition   Be bloody, bold and resolute. Laugh to scorn the power of man. Nobody born of woman shall harm Macbeth.

[*The* **Second Apparition** *goes*]

Macbeth   Then live, Macduff. Why need I fear you? But I'll make doubly sure, to back fate up. You must die. Then I can scorn the lies of my cowardly fear and sleep through thunder!

[*Thunder. A* **Third Apparition** *faces him – a child, crowned, with a tree in his hand*]

What's this, that looks like a royal child, wearing a king's crown on his infant head?

All   Listen, but speak not to't.

90 **3rd Apparition**   Be lion-mettled, proud, and take no care
Who chafes, who frets, or where conspirers are:
Macbeth shall never vanquished be until
Great Birnam wood to high Dunsinane hill
Shall come against him.

                                              [*Descends*]

Macbeth   That will never be;
95 Who can impress the forest, bid the tree
Unfix his earth-bound root? Sweet bodements! good.
Rebellious dead, rise never, till the wood
Of Birnam rise, and our high-placed Macbeth
Shall live the lease of nature, pay his breath
100 To time and mortal custom. Yet my heart
Throbs to know one thing; tell me, if your art
Can tell so much: shall Banquo's issue ever
Reign in this kingdom?

All   Seek to know no more.

Macbeth   I will be satisfied: deny me this,
105 And an eternal curse fall on you! Let me know –

[*The cauldron descends*]

Why sinks that cauldron? and what noise is this?

1st Witch   Show!

2nd Witch   Show!

3rd Witch   Show!

110 **All**   Show his eyes, and grieve his heart;
Come like shadows, so depart.

All   Listen, but don't speak to it!

3rd Apparition   Be brave as a lion, proud, and take no heed of those who vex or worry, or of where the plotters are. Macbeth shall never be vanquished till Great Birnam Wood advances against him to the high hill at Dunsinane.

[*It goes*]

Macbeth   That's never! Who can command a forest or order trees to leave the ground? That promises well. Good! Only when Birnam Wood arises, need I fear rebellions or the rising dead. Royal Macbeth will live his full life span, and die naturally from old age. Yet my heart yearns to know one thing. Tell me, if your skills extend that far: shall Banquo's offspring ever reign in this kingdom?

All   Don't try to know more!

Macbeth   I insist! Deny this to me, and may you be cursed eternally! Let me know!

[*The cauldron starts to sink, and trumpets sound*]

Why is the cauldron sinking? What's the noise?

1st Witch   Show!

2nd Witch   Show!

3rd Witch   Show!

All   Show his eyes, and grieve his heart;
Come like shadows. Then depart.

[*A show of eight* **Kings**, *the last with a glass in his hand;*
Banquo's Ghost *following.*]

Macbeth   Thou art too like the spirit of Banquo: down!
Thy crown does sear mine eye-balls. And thy hair,
Thou other gold-bound brow, is like the first.
115 A third is like the former. Filthy hags!
Why do you show me this? – A fourth? Start, eyes!
What, will the line stretch out to th' crack of doom?
Another yet? A seventh? I'll see no more:
And yet the eighth appears, who bears a glass
120 Which shows me many more; and some I see
That two-fold balls and treble sceptres carry.
Horrible sight! Now I see 'tis true,
For the blood-boltered Banquo smiles upon me,
And points at them for his. What, is this so?

125 **1st Witch**   Ay, sir, all this is so. But why
Stands Macbeth thus amazedly?
Come, sisters, cheer we up his sprites,
And show the best of our delights.
I'll charm the air to give a sound,
130 While you perform your antic round:
That this great king may kindly say
Our duties did his welcome pay.

[*Music. The* **Witches** *dance, and vanish.*]

Macbeth   Where are they? Gone? Let this pernicious hour
Stand aye accursed in the calendar
135 Come in, without there!

[*Enter* **Lennox**]

Lennox   What's your grace's will?

[*A procession of eight* **Kings** *appears, the last carrying a mirror, with* **Banquo** *following*]

Macbeth   [*To the first*] You are too like the ghost of Banquo! Down! Your crown blinds my eyes. [*To the second*] Your hair under your golden crown looks like the first's. [*To the third*] The third is like the others. [*To the* **Witches**] You filthy hags! Why are you showing me this? [*To the fourth*] Not a fourth? My eyes are strained. [*A fifth and sixth pass by*] What, will this line stretch out eternally? [*A seventh appears*] Yet another? A seventh? I won't look. [*But he keeps looking, in horror*] And now the eighth appears, carrying a mirror, showing me many more. Some coronation crowns combine two kingdoms! A ghastly sight! And I see it's the truth – blood-splattered Banquo smiles at me and points to the kings as his. What – is this so?

1st Witch   Yes, sir, all this is so. But why is Macbeth so amazed? Come, sisters, let's cheer up his sprites
By showing him our best delights.
I'll charm the air to give a sound
While you cavort and dance around,
So this great king may kindly say
His welcome got its rightful pay.

[*There is music, and the* **Witches** *dance. Then they vanish*]

Macbeth   Where are they? Gone? May this vile time be forever cursed in the calendar! [*He calls*] Come in, you outside there!

[**Lennox** *enters*]

Lennox   What can I do for Your Highness?

Macbeth   Saw you the Weird Sisters?

Lennox   No, my lord.

Macbeth   Came they not by you?

Lennox   No indeed, my lord.

Macbeth   Infected be the air whereon they ride,
    And damned all those that trust them! I did hear
140 The galloping of horse. Who was't came by?

  Lennox   'Tis two or three, my lord, that bring you word
    Macduff is fled to England.

Macbeth   Fled to England!

Lennox   Ay, my good lord.

Macbeth   Time, thou anticipat'st my dread exploits:
145 The flighty purpose never is o'ertook
    Unless the deed go with it. From this moment
    The very firstlings of my heart shall be
    The firstlings of my hand. And even now
    To crown my thoughts with acts, be it thought and done!
150 The castle of Macduff I will surprise,
    Seize upon Fife, give to th'edge o'th'sword
    His wife, his babes, and all unfortunate souls
    That trace him in his line. No boasting like a fool;
    This deed I'll do before this purpose cool.
155 But no more sights! Where are these gentlemen?
    Come, bring me where they are.

[*Exeunt*]

Macbeth   Did you see the Weird Sisters?

Lennox   No, my lord.

Macbeth   Didn't they pass you?

Lennox   No indeed, my lord.

Macbeth   May the air they ride on be infected! And damned be all those who trust them. I heard the galloping of horses. Who was it passed by?

Lennox   It is two or three, my lord, who bring you word that Macduff has fled to England.

Macbeth   Fled to England?

Lennox   Yes, my good lord.

Macbeth   Time, you are a step ahead of me in my scheming. Only when we act instantly do deeds keep pace with plans. Now, to unite thought and action, let this be thought and done. I'll take Macduff's castle by surprise. I'll occupy Fife and kill his wife, his children and all his relations. No boasting like a fool! This I'll do before my temper cools. But no more of those sights! [*To* **Lennox**] Where are these messengers? Come, take me to them.

[*They go*]

Scene 2

Fife. Macduff's castle. Enter **Lady Macduff**, *her* **Son**, *and* **Ross**.

Lady Macduff   What had he done, to make him fly the land?

Ross   You must have patience, madam.

Lady Macduff   He had none:
His flight was madness: when our actions do not,
Our fears do make us traitors.

Ross   You know not
5   Whether it was his wisdom or his fear.

Lady Macduff   Wisdom! to leave his wife, to leave his babes,
His mansion and his titles, in a place
From whence himself does fly? He loves us not;
He wants the natural touch: for the poor wren,
10   The most diminutive of birds, will fight,
Her young ones in her nest, against the owl.
All is the fear and nothing is the love;
As little is the wisdom, where the flight
So runs against all reason.

Ross   My dearest coz,
15   I pray you school yourself. But, for your husband,
He is noble, wise, judicious, and best knows
The fits o'th'season. I dare not speak much further,
But cruel are the times, when we are traitors
And do not know ourselves; when we hold rumour
20   From what we fear, yet know not what we fear,
But float upon a wild and violent sea,
Each way and more. I take my leave of you:
Shall not be long but I'll be here again:
Things at the worst will cease, or else climb upward
25   To what they were before. My pretty cousin,
Blessing upon you!

Scene 2

Macduff's *castle at Fife.* **Lady Macduff,** *her* **Son** *and* **Ross** *enter.*

Lady Macduff   What had he done, to make him leave the country?

Ross   You must have patience, madam.

Lady Macduff   He had none. His flight was madness. Fear makes us traitors even when our actions don't.

Ross   It might have been wisdom rather than fear.

Lady Macduff   Wisdom? To leave his wife, to leave his children, his house, his titles, in the very place he flies from? He doesn't love us. He lacks a parent's instinct. Even the poor wren, the tiniest of birds, will fight for her young ones in the nest against an owl. This is all fear: there's no element of love. No wisdom, either, where flight is against all common sense.

Ross   My dearest cousin, control yourself. Your husband is noble, wise, judicious and the best judge of present circumstances. I dare not elaborate. The times are cruel when we are traitors and don't know it. Fear breeds rumors, though what we fear is uncertain. We are tossed about this way and that, as if in a storm at sea. I'll say goodbye. I'll be back shortly. Trouble will either cease or build up again. My pretty cousin, bless you.

Lady Macduff   Fathered he is, and yet he's fatherless.

Ross   I am so much a fool, should I stay longer
It would be my disgrace and your discomfort.
30   I take my leave at once.

[*Exit*]

Lady Macduff   Sirrah, your father's dead,
And what will you do now? How will you live?

Son   As birds do, mother.

Lady Macduff   What, with worms and flies?

Son   With what I get, I mean, and so do they.

Lady Macduff   Poor bird! thou'ldst never fear the net nor
lime,
35   The pitfall nor the gin.

Son   Why should I, mother? Poor birds they are not set for.
My father is not dead, for all your saying.

Lady Macduff   Yes, he is dead: how wilt thou do for a father?

Son   Nay, how will you do for a husband?

40 **Lady Macduff**   Why, I can buy me twenty at any market.

Son   Then you'll buy'em to sell again.

Lady Macduff   Thou speak'st with all thy wit, and yet i'faith
With wit enough for thee.

Son   Was my father a traitor, mother?

45 **Lady Macduff**   Ay, that he was.

Son   What is a traitor?

Lady Macduff   Why, one that swears and lies.

148

Lady Macduff [*Looking at her son*] He has a fath‹
fatherless.

Ross If I stayed longer, my feelings would get the
to my disgrace and your embarrassment. I'll go now.

[**Ross** *leaves*]

Lady Macduff Son, your father's dead. And what will you do
now? How will you live?

Son As birds do, mother.

Lady Macduff What – on worms and flies?

Son On whatever I can get, I mean, as they do.

Lady Macduff Poor bird! Would you never fear the net, or
birdlime, traps or cages?

Son [*Joking*] Why should I, mother? They don't set traps for
poor birds! [*Seriously*] My father isn't dead, whatever you
say.

Lady Macduff Yes, he's dead. What will you do for a father?

Son Rather, what will you do for a husband?

Lady Macduff Why, I can buy myself twenty at any market.

Son Then you'll buy them to sell again?

Lady Macduff You speak as a child, but wittily enough!

Son Was my father a traitor, mother?

Lady Macduff Yes, that he was.

Son What is a traitor?

Lady Macduff Why, one who swears and lies.

Son   And be all traitors that do so?

Lady Macduff   Every one that does so is a traitor, and must be
hanged.

50 **Son**   And must they all be hanged that swear and lie?

Lady Macduff   Every one.

Son   Who must hang them?

Lady Macduff   Why, the honest men.

Son   Then the liars and swearers are fools; for there are liars
55   and swearers enow to beat the honest men and hang up them.

Lady Macduff   Now God help thee, poor monkey! But how
wilt thou do for a father?

Son   If he were dead, you'ld weep for him: if you would not, it
were a good sign that I should quickly have a new father.

60 **Lady Macduff**   Poor prattler, how thou talk'st!

[*Enter a* **Messenger**]

Messenger   Bless you, fair dame! I am not to you known,
Though in your state of honour I am perfect.
I doubt some danger does approach you nearly.
If you will take a homely man's advice,
65   Be not found here; hence, with your little ones.
To fright you thus, methinks I am too savage;
To do worse to you were fell cruelty,
Which is too nigh your person. Heaven preserve you!
I dare abide no longer.

[*Exit*]

Lady Macduff   Whither should I fly?
70   I have done no harm. But I remember now

Son   And are all who do so traitors?

Lady Macduff   Everyone who does so is a traitor and must be hanged.

Son   And must all who swear and lie be hanged?

Lady Macduff   Every one.

Son   Who must hang them?

Lady Macduff   Why, the honest men.

Son   Then the liars and swearers are fools. There are enough liars and swearers to beat the honest men and hang them!

Lady Macduff   Now heaven help you, you little monkey! [*She laughs but soon returns to her melancholy mood*] What will you do for a father?

Son   If he really were dead, you'd weep for him – and if you didn't weep, I'd know I would be getting a new father soon.

Lady Macduff   Chatterbox! How you do talk!

[*A* **Messenger** *enters*]

Messenger   Bless you, fair madam. You don't know me, but I know you well enough. I think you are very close to danger. If you will take a humble man's advice, don't be found here. Go with your little ones. It's brutal of me to frighten you like this, but I'd be more cruel if I did less, and cruelty is not far away. Heaven help you! I daren't stay any longer.

[*He goes*]

Lady Macduff   Where should I go? I've done no harm. But now I remember – I'm on this earth, where to do harm is

151

I am in this earthly world; where to do harm
Is often laudable, to do good sometime
Accounted dangerous folly: why then, alas,
Do I put up that womanly defence,
To say I have done no harm?

[*Enter* **Murderers**]

75   What are these faces?

Murderer   Where is your husband?

Lady Macduff   I hope, in no place so unsanctified
Where such as thou mayst find him.

Murderer   He's a traitor.

Son   Thou liest, thou shag-haired villain.

80 **Murderer**   What, you egg!
Young fry of treachery!   [*Stabs him*]

Son   He has killed me, mother:
Run away, I pray you.   [*Dies*]

[*Exit* **Lady Macduff** *crying 'murder', pursued by the*
Murderers.]

Scene 3

England. Before the King's palace. Enter **Malcolm** *and* **Macduff**.

Malcolm   Let us seek out some desolate shade, and there
Weep our sad bosoms empty.

Macduff   Let us rather
Hold fast the mortal sword, and like good men

praiseworthy and to do good is dangerous stupidity. Why then do I put up that womanly defense, "I've done no harm"?

[**Murderers** *enter*]

Who are these people?

1st Murderer   Where is your husband?

Lady Macduff   I hope in no place so unholy that such as you might find him.

1st Murderer   He's a traitor.

Son   You're lying, you longhaired ruffian!

1st Murderer   What, you spawn! You little offspring of treachery!

[*He stabs him*]

Son   He's killed me, mother! Run away, I beg you!

[*He dies*]

[**Lady Macduff,** *screaming "Murder, murder!" runs off pursued by the* **Murderers**]

Scene 3

England, near the palace of Edward the Confessor. **Malcolm** *and* **Macduff** *enter.*

Malcolm   Let's find some lonely, shady spot and there weep away our sadness.

Macduff   Far better to take up arms, like worthy men, in

Bestride our down-fall'n birthdom: each new morn
5 New widows howl, new orphans cry, new sorrows
Strike heaven on the face, that it resounds
As if it felt with Scotland and yelled out
Like syllable of dolour.

Malcolm   What I believe, I'll wail;
What know, believe; and what I can redress,
10 As I shall find the time to friend, I will.
What you have spoke, it may be so perchance.
This tyrant, whose sole name blisters our tongues,
Was once thought honest: you have loved him well;
He hath not touched you yet. I am young, but something
15 You may deserve of him through me; and wisdom
To offer up a weak, poor, innocent lamb,
T'appease an angry god.

Macduff   I am not treacherous.

Malcolm   But Macbeth is.
A good and virtuous nature may recoil
20 In an imperial charge. But I shall crave your pardon;
That which you are, my thoughts cannot transpose:
Angels are bright still, though the brightest fell:
Though all things foul would wear the brows of grace,
Yet grace must still look so.

Macduff   I have lost my hopes.

25 **Malcolm**   Perchance even there where I did find my doubts.
Why in that rawness left you wife and child,
Those precious motives, those strong knots of love,
Without leave-taking? I pray you,
Let not my jealousies be your dishonours,
30 But mine own safeties: you may be rightly just,
Whatever I shall think.

defense of our motherland. Every day, new widows mourn, new orphans cry, new sorrows strike Heaven in the face. Heaven groans in sympathy with Scotland and weeps for its suffering.

Malcolm What I believe, I'll mourn. What I know, I'll believe. What I can, I'll put right when the time is right. What you have said may well be true. This tyrant, whose very name blisters our tongues, was once thought honest. You loved him well. He hasn't touched you yet. I'm young, but by betraying me you could do yourself some good. It's wise policy to sacrifice a weak, poor, innocent lamb to appease an angry god!

Macduff I'm not treacherous.

Malcolm But Macbeth is. Even a good and virtuous nature can be forgiven for yielding to pressure from a king. Forgive me. My wishful thinking can't change what you really are. Angels are still bright although the brightest fell. All wickedness tries to look like virtue. Yet virtue itself can't change.

Macduff I have lost hope.

Malcolm Perhaps that's why I am so suspicious. Why did you leave your wife and child so vulnerable? Your most precious possessions, bound with knots of love? Why no farewells? Please – I wouldn't wish my suspicions to dishonor you. They're for my own safety. You may well be honorable, whatever I may think.

Macduff   Bleed, bleed, poor country!
Great tyranny, lay thou thy basis sure,
For goodness dares not check thee: wear thou thy wrongs,
The title is affeered! Fare thee well, lord:
35   I would not be the villain that thou think'st
For the whole space that's in the tyrant's grasp,
And the rich East to boot.

Malcolm   Be not offended:
I speak not as in absolute fear of you:
    I think our country sinks beneath the yoke,
40   It weeps, it bleeds, and each new day a gash
Is added to her wounds I think withal
There would be hands uplifted in my right;
And here from gracious England have I offer
Of goodly thousands. But for all this,
45   When I shall tread upon the tyrant's head,
Or wear it on my sword, yet my poor country
Shall have more vices than it had before,
More suffer and more sundry ways than ever,
By him that shall succeed.

Macduff   What should he be?

50 **Malcolm**   It is myself I mean: in whom I know
All the particulars of vice so grafted
That, when they shall be opened, black Macbeth
Will seem as pure as snow, and the poor state
Esteem him as a lamb, being compared
55   With my confineless harms.

Macduff   Not in the legions
Of horrid hell can come a devil more damned
In evils to top Macbeth.

Malcolm   I grant him bloody,
Luxurious, avaricious, false, deceitful,
Sudden, malicious, smacking of every sin

Macduff   [*Overcome*] Bleed, bleed, poor country! Tyranny –
build strong foundations: goodness dares not stop you. Wear
your ill-gotten crown: the law's behind you. Farewell, lord. I
wouldn't be the villain that you think me for all the tyrant's
territories – and the rich East as well!

Malcolm   Don't be offended. I don't distrust you totally. I think
our country is oppressed. It weeps. It bleeds. Every new day, a
gash is added to her wounds. Nevertheless, I think there
would be many who'd fight my cause. The gracious king of
England offered several thousand men. But for all this, when I
have the tyrant's head beneath my foot – or on my sword –
my poor country will have more vices than it had before. It will
suffer more, and in many more ways, under the new king.

Macduff   Who will that be?

Malcolm   I mean myself. In me, I know vice is so rooted that
when I blossom forth, black Macbeth will seem as pure as
snow. The poor country will regard him as a lamb in
comparison with my infinite evil.

Macduff   Not in the ranks of horrid hell could there come a devil
more damned in evils than Macbeth!

Malcolm   I grant you he's murderous, lustful, greedy,
treacherous, deceitful, impetuous, malicious and smacking
of every sin that has a name. But there's no limit – none – to

60   That has a name: but there's no bottom, none,
     In my voluptuousness: your wives, your daughters,
     Your matrons and your maids, could not fill up
     The cistern of my lust, and my desire
     All continent impediments would o'erbear
65   That did oppose my will. Better Macbeth,
     Than such an one to reign.

Macduff   Boundless intemperance
     In nature is a tyranny; it hath been
     Th'untimely emptying of the happy throne,
     And fall of many kings. But fear not yet
70   To take upon you that is yours: you may
     Convey your pleasures in a spacious plenty,
     And yet seem cold, the time you may so hoodwink:
     We have willing dames enough; there cannot be
     That vulture in you, to devour so many
75   As will to greatness dedicate themselves,
     Finding it so inclined.

Malcolm   With this there grows
     In my most ill-composed affection such
     A stanchless avarice that, were I king,
     I should cut off the nobles for their lands,
80   Desire his jewels and this other's house,
     And my more-having would be as a sauce
     To make me hunger more, that I should forge
     Quarrels unjust against the good and loyal,
     Destroying them for wealth.

Macduff   This avarice
85   Sticks deeper: grows with more pernicious root
     Than summer-seeming lust: and it hath been
     The sword of our slain kings: yet do not fear;
     Scotland hath foisons to fill up your will
     Of your mere own. All these are portable,
90   With other graces weighed.

my lust. Your wives, your daughters, your married women and your virgins – they couldn't satisfy my appetite. My passion would brook no opposition. Better Macbeth should reign than a man like that.

Macduff   An unbridled sexual appetite can tyrannize a man. It has caused many kings to fall and lose their thrones. But don't be afraid to take on what is yours. There's plenty of scope for you to indulge your pleasures secretly and still seem chaste. You can easily cover things up: there are plenty of willing wenches. The supply of obliging maidens must far exceed even your appetite.

Malcolm   As well as this, among my evil qualities is an insatiable greed. If I were king, I'd execute the nobles for their lands and desire this man's jewels, that man's house. The more I had, the more I'd hunger for – so much so, I'd invent unjust quarrels against the good and loyal, and destroy them for their wealth.

Macduff   This greed goes deeper. It has a firmer root system than short-lived lust. It has been the death of many of our kings. Yet do not fear. Scotland has rich harvests to satisfy your needs, within your own estates. All these faults are tolerable, weighed against other virtues.

Malcolm   But I have none. The king-becoming graces,
As justice, verity, temp'rance, stableness,
Bounty, perseverance, mercy, lowliness,
Devotion, patience, courage, fortitude,
95   I have no relish of them, but abound
In the division of each several crime,
Acting it many ways. Nay, had I power, I should
Pour the sweet milk of concord into hell,
Uproot the universal peace, confound
100   All unity on earth.

Macduff   O Scotland! Scotland!

Malcolm   If such a one be fit to govern, speak:
I am as I have spoken.

Macduff   Fit to govern!
No, not to live. O nation miserable!
With an untitled tyrant bloody-sceptred,
105   When shalt thou see thy wholesome days again,
Since that the truest issue of thy throne
By his own interdiction stands accurst,
And does blaspheme his breed? Thy royal father
Was a most sainted king; the queen that bore thee
110   Oft'ner upon her knees than on her feet,
Died every day she lived. Fare thee well!
These evils thou repeat'st upon thyself
Hath banished me from Scotland. O my breast,
Thy hope ends here!

Malcolm   Macduff, this noble passion,
115   Child of integrity, hath from my soul
Wiped the black scruples, reconciled my thoughts
To thy good truth and honour. Devilish Macbeth
By many of these trains hath sought to win me
Into his power; and modest wisdom plucks me
120   From over-credulous haste: but God above

Malcolm   But I have none. Virtues that become a king – justice, truth, temperance, stability, generosity, perseverance, mercy, humility, devotion, patience, courage, constancy – I have no trace of them. I wallow in the finer points of crime, in all its various roles. No. If I had power, toleration could go to hell. I'd play havoc with peace. I'd destroy all unity on earth.

Macduff   Oh, Scotland, Scotland!

Malcolm   If such a man is fit to govern, say so. I am what I've said I am.

Macduff   Fit to govern? No, not to live! Oh, wretched nation! With a usurping murderous tyrant on the throne, when will you see decent days again? The rightful heir stands self-accused of wickedness, blaspheming his ancestry. Your royal father was a most saintly king. The queen, your mother, more often on her knees in prayer than on her feet, was grave in thought every day of her life. Farewell. The evils you tell against yourself have banished me from Scotland. Oh, my heart! There is no hope!

Malcolm   Macduff, this noble passion – proof of your integrity – has wiped all black suspicions from my soul and satisfied my mind as to your truth and honor. By many such ruses, devilish Macbeth has tried to trick me into his power. Simple wisdom forbids me to be persuaded easily. But as God is our

Deal between thee and me! for even now
I put myself to thy direction, and
Unspeak mine own detraction; her abjure
The taints and blames I laid upon myself,
125 For strangers to my nature. I am yet
Unknown to woman, never was forsworn,
Scarcely have coveted what was mine own,
At no time broke my faith, would not betray
The devil to his fellow, and delight
130 No less in truth than life: my first false speaking
Was this upon myself: what I am truly
Is thine and my poor country's to command:
Whither indeed, before thy here-approach,
Old Siward, with ten thousand warlike men,
135 Already at a point, was setting forth.
Now we'll together, and the chance of goodness
Be like our warranted quarrel! Why are you silent?

Macduff Such welcome and unwelcome things at once
'Tis hard to reconcile.

[*Enter a* **Doctor**]

140 **Malcolm** Well, more anon. Comes the king forth, I pray you?

Doctor Ay, sir: there are a crew of wretched souls
That stay his cure: their malady convinces
The great assay of art; but at his touch,
Such sanctity hath heaven given his hand,
145 They presently amend.

Malcolm   I thank you, doctor.

[*Exit* **Doctor**]

Macduff What's the disease he means?

witness, I shall be guided by you and withdraw my words of
self-abuse: I renounce the stains and blemishes I said I had.
They are alien to my nature. I've never had a woman, never
gone back on my word. I've barely wanted what belongs to
me. At no time have I broken faith. I wouldn't betray the devil
to a fellow-fiend, and I love truth as much as life. My first lie
was my lie against myself. The real me is yours and my
poor country's to command. Indeed, before your arrival, old
Siward with ten thousand warlike soldiers, fully equipped,
was about to set out. Now we'll go together. Our hopes of
success match the justice of our cause. Why are you silent?

Macduff   It's hard to reconcile such welcome and unwelcome
things together.

[*A* **Doctor** *enters*]

Malcolm   Well, more later. Is King Edward coming out, may I
ask?

Doctor   Yes, sir. A crowd of wretched people seek his cure.
Their illnesses defy the skills of medicine. But at his touch,
such holiness has God given his hand, they are soon cured.

Malcolm   I thank you, doctor.

[*The* **Doctor** *goes*]

Macduff   What's the disease he means?

Malcolm   'Tis called the evil:
A most miraculous work in this good king,
Which often, since my here-remain in England,
I have seen him do. How he solicits heaven,
150   Himself best knows: but strangely-visited people,
All swoln and ulcerous, pitiful to the eye,
The mere despair of surgery, he cures,
Hanging a golden stamp about their necks,
Put on with holy prayers: and 'tis spoken,
155   To the succeeding royalty he leaves
The healing benediction. With this strange virtue
He hath a heavenly gift of prophecy,
And sundry blessings hang about his throne
That speak him full of grace.

[*Enter* **Ross**]

Macduff   See, who comes here.

160 **Malcolm**   My countryman; but yet I know him not.

Macduff   My ever-gentle cousin, welcome hither.

Malcolm   I know him now: good God, betimes remove
The means that makes us strangers!

Ross   Sir, amen.

Macduff   Stands Scotland where it did?

Ross   Alas, poor country,
165   Almost afraid to know itself. It cannot
Be called our mother, but our grave; where nothing,
But who knows nothing, is once seen to smile;
Where sighs and groans and shrieks that rend the air,
Are made, not marked; where violent sorrow seems
170   A modern ecstasy: the dead man's knell
Is there scarce asked for who, and good men's lives

Malcolm   It's called the King's Evil. It's a most miraculous gift the king has. I've often seen him use it since I came to England. Heaven and he alone best know the secret. He cures people with strange ailments – all swollen and ulcerous, pitiful to the eye and the total despair of surgeons. He hangs a golden coin around their necks while praying. It's said he'll pass on this healing gift to his royal successors. As well as this remarkable skill, he has a divine gift of prophecy. His reign is blessed. He is full of grace.

[**Ross** *enters*]

Macduff   Look who's here!

Malcolm   A fellow-countryman, but I do not know him.

Macduff   My kind cousin: welcome here.

Malcolm   I recognize him now. May the good lord soon remove the reason why we're strangers!

Ross   Amen to that.

Macduff   Is Scotland just the same?

Ross   Alas, poor country, it hardly knows itself. It can't be called our motherland. It's more our grave. Only those in ignorance can smile. Sighs, groans and shrieks go unheeded. Violence and sorrow are everyday experiences. Nobody asks for whom

Expire before the flowers in their caps,
Dying or ere they sicken.

Macduff   O, relation
Too nice, and yet too true!

Malcolm   What's the newest grief?

175 **Ross**   That of an hour's age doth hiss the speaker;
Each minute teems a new one.

Macduff   How does my wife?

Ross   Why, well.

Macduff   And all my children?

Ross   Well too.

Macduff   The tyrant has not battered at their peace?

Ross   No, they were well at peace, when I did leave 'em.

180 **Macduff**   Be not a niggard of your speech: how goes't?

Ross   When I came hither to transport the tidings
Which I have heavily borne, there ran a rumour
Of many worthy fellows that were out;
Which was to my belief witnessed the rather,
185 For that I saw the tyrant's power a-foot.
Now is the time of help: your eye in Scotland
Would create soldiers, make our women fight,
To doff their dire distresses.

Malcolm   Be't their comfort
We are coming thither: gracious England hath
190 Lent us good Siward and ten thousand men;
An older and a better soldier none
That Christendom gives out.

Ross   Would I could answer
This comfort with the like! But I have words,

the funeral bell tolls. Good men live lives shorter than the flowers in their caps; they die before their time.

Macduff   How sharply observed, and all too true!

Malcolm   What's the latest grief?

Ross   That of an hour ago is stale news. New bad news happens by the minute.

Macduff   How is my wife?

Ross   Why, well . . .

Macduff   And all my children?

Ross   Well too. . . .

Macduff   The tyrant has left them in peace?

Ross   They were well at peace when I left them.

Macduff   Tell us more. How are things going?

Ross   As I came here to deliver my depressing news, it was rumored that many worthy men were up in arms. This I could well believe as I saw the tyrant's forces on the march. We need your help now. Your appearance in Scotland would guarantee an army. Even our women would fight to shed their desperate misfortunes.

Malcolm   Let them take comfort. We are going there. The gracious Edward has lent us good Siward and ten thousand men. There's no more experienced or better soldier in Christendom.

Ross   I wish I could return your comfort. But I have news fit

That would be howled out in the desert air,
195   Where hearing should not latch them.

Macduff   What concern they?
The general cause? or is it a fee-grief
Due to some single breast?

Ross   No mind that's honest
But in it shares some woe, though the main part
Pertains to you alone.

Macduff   If it be mine,
200   Keep it not from me, quickly let me have it.

Ross   Let not your ears despise my tongue for ever,
Which shall possess them with the heaviest sound
That ever yet they heard.

Macduff   Hum! I guess at it.

Ross   Your castle is surprised; your wife and babes
205   Savagely slaughtered: to relate the manner,
Were, on the quarry of these murdered deer,
To add the death of you.

Malcolm   Merciful heaven!
What, man! ne'er pull your hat upon your brows;
Give sorrow words: the grief that does not speak
210   Whispers the o'er-fraught heart and bids it break.

Macduff   My children too?

Ross   Wife, children, servants, all
That could be found.

Macduff   And I must be from thence!
My wife killed too?

Ross   I have said.

only for howling to the desert air, where nobody could hear it.

Macduff   About what? Public affairs? Or someone's private grief?

Ross   Every decent man would share the woe, though it mainly relates to you alone.

Macduff   If it's mine, don't keep it from me. Quickly, let me have it.

Ross   Your ears may well despise my tongue forever. They will hear the saddest sound they ever yet have heard.

Macduff   Hmm . . . I think I can guess . . .

Ross   Your castle has been taken, your wife and children savagely slaughtered. To say how would be to add your death to those of your loved ones.

Malcolm   Merciful heaven! [*To* **Macduff**] What, man! Don't pull your hat down over your eyes! Say what you feel. Silent grief breaks the heart.

Macduff   My children too?

Ross   Wife, children, servants. All who could be found.

Macduff   And I had to be away! My wife killed too?

Ross   So I said.

Malcolm   Be comforted:
   Let's make us med'cines of our great revenge,
215   To cure this deadly grief.

   Macduff   He has no children. All my pretty ones?
   Did you say all? O, hell-kite! All?
   What, all my pretty chickens and their dam
   At one fell swoop?

220   **Malcolm**   Dispute it like a man.

   Macduff   I shall do so;
   But I must also feel it as a man:
   I cannot but remember such things were,
   That were most precious to me. Did heaven look on,
   And would not take their part? Sinful Macduff,
225   They were all struck for thee! naught that I am,
   Not for their own demerits, but for mine,
   Fell slaughter on their souls: heaven rest them now!

   Malcolm   Be this the whetstone of your sword: let grief
   Convert to anger; blunt not the heart, enrage it.

230   **Macduff**   O, I could play the woman with mine eyes,
   And braggart with my tongue! But, gentle heavens,
   Cut short all intermission; front to front
   Bring thou this fiend of Scotland and myself;
   Within my sword's length set him; if he 'scape,
235   Heaven forgive him too!

   Malcolm   This tune goes manly.
   Come, go we to the king, our power is ready,
   Our lack is nothing but our leave. Macbeth
   Is ripe for shaking, and the powers above
   Put on their instruments. Receive what cheer you may;
240   The night is long that never finds the day.

                                                    [*Exeunt*]

Malcolm   Take comfort. We'll make our great revenge the medicine to cure this deadly grief.

Macduff   He has no children! All my pretty ones? Did you say "all"? All? All? Oh, the fiend! All? What, all my pretty chickens and their mother at one fell swoop?

Malcolm   Face it like a man.

Macduff   I'll do that. But I must also feel it like a man. I can't forget what was so precious to me. Did Heaven witness this and not defend them? Sinful Macduff! They were killed for you! Worthless as I am, they died for my sins, not their own. May they rest in peace!

Malcolm   Let this sharpen your sword. Let grief turn to anger. Don't let your spirit flag – bestir it!

Macduff   Oh, I could weep like a woman and rant with my tongue! But gentle heavens, let there be no delay! Bring this fiend of Scotland and myself face-to-face! Put him at a sword's length before me. If he should escape, we'd both need heaven's forgiveness!

Malcolm   Spoken like a man. Let's go to the king. Our army is ready. We need to do nothing but take our leave. Macbeth is ripe for toppling, and the powers above will find the means. Take comfort from this fact: It's a long night that has no dawn.

[*They go*]

Act five

Scene 1

Dunsinane. A room in the castle. Enter a **Doctor of Physic**, *and a* **Waiting Gentlewoman**.

Doctor   I have two nights watched with you, but can perceive no truth in your report. When was it she last walked?

Gentlewoman   Since his majesty went into the field, I have seen her rise from her bed, throw her night-gown upon her,
5   unlock her closet, take forth paper, fold it, write upon't, read it, afterwards seal it, and again return to bed; yet all this while in a most fast sleep.

Doctor   A great perturbation in nature, to receive at once the benefit of sleep and do the effects of watching! In this
10   slumbery agitation, besides her walking and other actual performances, what, at any time, have you heard her say?

Gentlewoman   That, sir, which I will not report after her.

Doctor   You may to me, and 'tis most meet you should.

Gentlewoman   Neither to you nor any one, having no witness
15   to confirm my speech.

[*Enter* **Lady Macbeth**, *with a taper*]

Lo you, here she comes! This is her very guise, and upon my life fast asleep. Observe her, stand close.

Doctor   How came she by that light?

Gentlewoman   Why, it stood by her: she has light by her
20   continually, 'tis her command.

Act five

Scene 1

A room in the castle at Dunsinane. A **Doctor** *and a* **Lady-in-Waiting** *enter.*

Doctor I've watched with you for two nights, but I can see no truth in your story. When was it she last walked?

Lady Since His Majesty went to war, I have seen her rise from her bed, throw on a nightgown, unlock her strongbox, take out a paper, fold it, write upon it, read it, then seal it and return to bed again. And all this while fast asleep.

Doctor Very unnatural, to have the benefit of sleep at the same time as performing the tasks of wakefulness. In this restless sleep, besides her walking about and other observable actions, what, at any time, have you heard her say?

Lady Things, sir, that I won't repeat after her.

Doctor You can to me. It's most proper that you should.

Lady Neither to you nor to anyone, since I have no witness to confirm what I say.

[**Lady Macbeth** *enters with a candle*]

Look, here she comes! This is her usual style, and upon my life she's fast asleep. Watch her, and keep hidden.

Doctor How did she get the light?

Lady Why, it was at her bedside. She has light by her continually. It's her orders.

Doctor   You see, her eyes are open.

Gentlewoman   Ay, but their sense are shut.

Doctor   What is it she does now? Look, how she rubs her
hands.

25 **Gentlewoman**   It is an accustomed action with her, to seem
thus washing her hands: I have known her continue in this a
quarter of an hour.

Lady Macbeth   Yet here's a spot.

Doctor   Hark, she speaks! I will set down what comes from
30   her, to satisfy my remembrance the more strongly.

Lady Macbeth   Out, damned spot! out, I say! One: two: why,
then 'tis time to do't. Hell is murky! Fie, my lord, fie! a
soldier, and afeard? What need we fear who knows it, when
none can call our power to accompt? Yet who would have
35   thought the old man to have had so much blood in him?

Doctor   Do you mark that?

Lady Macbeth   The Thane of Fife had a wife; where is she
now? What, will these hands ne'er be clean? No more o'that,
my lord, no more o'that: you mar all with this starting.

40 **Doctor**   Go to, go to; you have known what you should not.

Gentlewoman   She has spoke what she should not, I am sure
of that: heaven knows what she has known.

Lady Macbeth   Here's the smell of the blood still: all the
perfumes of Arabia will not sweeten this little hand. Oh! oh!
45   oh!

Doctor   What a sigh is there! The heart is sorely charged.

Gentlewoman   I would not have such a heart in my bosom, for
the dignity of the whole body.

Doctor   You see, her eyes are open!

Lady   Yes, but they do not really see.

Doctor   What's she doing now? Look how she rubs her hands.

Lady   It's a habit with her, to seem to wash her hands. I've known her to do this for a quarter of an hour.

Lady Macbeth   Yet here's a spot!

Doctor   Listen, she's speaking! I'll write down what she says, to reinforce my memory.

Lady Macbeth   Out, damned spot! Out, I say! [*She remembers the bell she struck on the night of Duncan's murder*] One. Two. Why, now's the time to do it. [*She shudders*] Hell is murky! [*Returning to her past conversations*] Control yourself, my lord! A soldier, and frightened? Why should we fear who knows it, when no one can challenge our authority? Yet who would have thought the old man had so much blood in him?

Doctor   Did you note that?

Lady Macbeth   The thane of Fife had a wife. Where is she now? [*Rubbing her hands*] What, will these hands never be clean? [*As if at the banquet*] Less of that, my lord, less of that! You spoil everything with this panicking!

Doctor   Come now: you've found out what you shouldn't.

Lady   She has spoken what she shouldn't, I'm sure of that. God knows what she knows.

Lady Macbeth   [*Her hand to her nose*] The smell of the blood is still there. All the perfumes of Arabia cannot sweeten this little hand. [*She sighs deeply*] Oh, oh, oh!

Doctor   What a sigh that was! Her heart is heavy-burdened.

Lady   I wouldn't have a heart like that in my bosom, for all her queenly rank.

Doctor   Well, well, well, –

50 **Gentlewoman**   Pray God it be, sir.

Doctor   This disease is beyond my practice: yet I have known
those which have walked in their sleep who have died holily in
their beds.

Lady Macbeth   Wash your hands, put on your night-gown,
55   look not so pale: I tell you yet again, Banquo's buried; he
cannot come out on's grave.

Doctor   Even so?

Lady Macbeth   To bed, to bed: there's knocking at the gate:
come, come, come, come, give me your hand: what's done,
60   cannot be undone: to bed, to bed, to bed.

[*Exit*]

Doctor   Will she go now to bed?

Gentlewoman   Directly.

Doctor   Foul whisp'rings are abroad: unnatural deeds
Do breed unnatural troubles: infected minds
65   To their deaf pillows will discharge their secrets:
More needs she the divine than the physician
God, God forgive us all! Look after her,
Remove from her the means of all annoyance,
And still keep eyes upon her. So, good night:
70   My mind she has mated and amazed my sight:
I think, but dare not speak.

Gentlewoman   Good night, good doctor.

[*Exeunt*]

176

Doctor   Well, well, well . . .

Lady   I pray to God it is well, sir!

Doctor   This disease is beyond my skill. Yet I've known people who've walked in their sleep who have died holily in their beds.

Lady Macbeth   [*Going over the past*] Wash your hands. Put on your nightgown. Don't look so pale. I tell you yet again: Banquo is buried. He can't rise from his grave.

Doctor   [*Realizing the truth*] So that's it?

Lady Macbeth   To bed, to bed. There's someone knocking at the gate. Come, come, come, come. Give me your hand. What's done cannot be undone. To bed, to bed, to bed.

[*She goes*]

Doctor   Will she go to bed now?

Lady   Right away.

Doctor   Vile rumors circulate. Unnatural deeds breed unnatural troubles. Disturbed minds confide their secrets to their deaf pillows. She needs a priest more than she needs a doctor. God, God forgive us all. Look after her. Take all harmful things away from her. And continue to keep your eyes on her. So, goodnight. She has confounded my mind and amazed my sight. I have my thoughts but daren't speak them.

Lady   Goodnight, doctor.

[*They go*]

Scene 2

The country near Dunsinane. Drum and colours. Enter **Menteith,
Caithness, Angus, Lennox,** *and* **Soldiers.**

Menteith   The English power is near, led on by Malcolm,
His uncle Siward and the good Macduff.
Revenges burn in them: for their dear causes
Would to the bleeding and the grim alarm
5   Excite the mortified man.

Angus   Near Birnam wood
Shall we meet them, and that way are they coming.

Caithness   Who knows if Donalbain be with his brother?

Lennox   For certain, sir, he is not: I have a file
Of all the gentry: there is Siward's son,
10   And many unrough youths, that even now
Protest their first of manhood.

Menteith   What does the tyrant?

Caithness   Great Dunsinane he strongly fortifies:
Some say he's mad; others, that lesser hate him,
Do call it valiant fury: but, for certain,
15   He cannot buckle his distempered cause
Within the belt of rule.

Angus   Now does he feel
His secret murders sticking on his hands;
Now minutely revolts upbraid his faith-breach;
Those he commands move only in command,
20   Nothing in love: now does he feel his title
Hang loose about him, like a giant's robe
Upon a dwarfish thief.

Scene 2

The open country near Dunsinane. Drums are heard and flags are flying. **Menteith, Caithness, Angus, Lennox,** *and* **Soldiers** *enter.*

Menteith   The English army is near, led by Malcolm, his uncle Siward and the good Macduff. They burn for revenge. Their just cause urges them to battle. The call to arms would stir the dead.

Angus   We shall probably meet them near Birnam Wood. They are coming that way.

Caithness   Does anyone know if Donalbain is with his brother?

Lennox   Sir, he is definitely not. I've a list of all the gentry. There's Siward's son, as well as many youngsters asserting their manhood for the first time.

Menteith   What's the tyrant doing?

Caithness   He has strongly fortified the castle at Dunsinane. Some say he's mad. Others who hate him less call it "valiant fury." One thing's certain: he's lost all self-control.

Angus   Now he feels his secret murders sticking on his hands. Now, every minute, revolts revenge his crimes. Those he commands obey from duty, not love. Now he feels his royalty sagging about him, like a giant's robe on a dwarf-sized thief.

Menteith   Who then shall blame
His pestered senses to recoil and start,
When all that is within him does condemn
25 Itself for being there?

Caithness   Well, march we on,
To give obedience where 'tis truly owed:
Meet we the med'cine of the sickly weal,
And with him pour we, in our country's purge,
Each drop of us.

Lennox   Or so much as it needs
30 To dew the sovereign flower and drown the weeds.
Make we our march towards Birnam.

[*Exeunt, marching*]

Scene 3

Dunsinane. A court in the castle. Enter **Macbeth, Doctor,** *and*
Attendants.

Macbeth   Bring me no more reports, let them fly all:
Till Birnam wood remove to Dunsinane
I cannot taint with fear. What's the boy Malcolm?
Was he not born of woman? The spirits that know
5 All mortal consequence have pronounced me thus:
'Fear not, Macbeth, no man that's born of woman
Shall e'er have power upon thee'. Then fly, false thanes,
And mingle with the English epicures:
The mind I sway by and the heart I bear
10 Shall never sag with doubt nor shake with fear.

Menteith   Who can blame his tattered nerves for being shaken, when his mind is ashamed of being part of him?

Caithness   Well, let's march on, to give service where it's properly due. Let's meet our ailing country's doctor – Malcolm – and with him shed every last drop of our blood to purify our land of its sickness.

Lennox   Or as much of it as we need to water the flower of kingship but drown the weeds! Let us march on to Birnam!

[*They march off*]

Scene 3

A court in the castle at Dunsinane. **Macbeth,** *the* **Doctor** *and* **Attendants** *enter.*

Macbeth   Bring me no more reports! Those cowards can all run away. Till Birnam Wood comes to Dunsinane, I have no fear. Who's this lad Malcolm? Wasn't he born of woman? The spirits that know our life spans told me this: "Fear not, Macbeth. No man that's born of woman shall ever have power over you." So run, you false thanes, and mix with the English degenerates! *My* mind and *my* courage will never droop with doubt or shake with fear!

[*Enter a* **Servant**]

The devil damn thee black, thou cream-faced loon!
Where got'st thou that goose look?

Servant   There is ten thousand –

Macbeth   Geese, villain?

Servant   Soldiers, sir.

Macbeth   Go prick thy face and over-red thy fear,
15   Thou lily-livered boy. What soldiers, patch?
Death of thy soul! those linen cheeks of thine
Are counsellors to fear. What soldiers, whey-face?

Servant   The English force, so please you.

Macbeth   Take thy face hence.

[*Exit* **Servant**]

Seton! – I am sick at heart
20   When I behold – Seton, I say! – This push
Will cheer me ever, or disseat me now.
I have lived long enough: my way of life
Is fall'n into the sere, the yellow leaf,
And that which should accompany old age,
25   As honour, love, obedience, troops of friends,
I must not look to have; but, in their stead,
Curses, not loud but deep, mouth-honour, breath
Which the poor heart would fain deny and dare not.
Seton!

Enter **Seton**

30 **Seton**   What is your gracious pleasure?

Macbeth   What news more?

[*A* **Servant** *enters*]

May the devil turn you black, you pale-faced lunatic! Where did you get that goose look?

Servant   There are ten thousand –

Macbeth   Geese, villain?

Servant   Soldiers, sir.

Macbeth   Go pinch your face and redden over your fear, you lily-livered boy! What soldiers, fool? By the death of your soul, those pallid cheeks of yours encourage fear! What soldiers, you palefaced one?

Servant   The English army, so please you.

Macbeth   Go away!

[*The* **Servant** *runs off*]

[*Calling*] Seton! [*Dejectedly*] I'm sick at heart when I see – [*Without finishing his sentence he shouts again angrily*] Seton, I say! [*Resuming his thoughts*] This is the conflict that will make or break me. I have lived long enough. My pathway of life has reached the withered state, its autumn. What should accompany old age – such as honor, love, obedience, troops of friends – I cannot hope to have. Instead I'll have curses, not spoken aloud, but deeply felt; lip service; courtesies uttered out of fear, not heartfelt. Seton!

[**Seton** *answers the call*]

Seton   What is Your Highness's pleasure?

Macbeth   What's the latest news?

Seton   All is confirmed, my lord, which was reported.

Macbeth   I'll fight, till from my bones my flesh be hacked.
Give me my armour.

Seton   'Tis not needed yet.

Macbeth   I'll put it on.
35 Send out more horses, skirr the country round,
Hang those talk of fear. Give me mine armour.
How goes your patient, Doctor?

Doctor   Not so sick, my lord,
As she is troubled with thick-coming fancies,
That keep her from her rest.

Macbeth   Cure her of that:
40 Canst thou not minister to a mind diseased,
Pluck from the memory a rooted sorrow,
Raze out the written troubles of the brain,
And with some sweet oblivious antidote
Cleanse the stuffed bosom of that perilous stuff
45 Which weighs upon the heart?

Doctor   Therein the patient
Must minister to himself.

Macbeth   Throw physic to the dogs, I'll none of it.
Come, put mine armour on; give me my staff;
Seton, send out; Doctor, the thanes fly from me;
50 Come, sir, dispatch. – If thou couldst, Doctor, cast
The water of my land, find her disease,
And purge it to a sound and pristine health,
I would applaud thee to the very echo
That should applaud again. – Pull't off, I say. –
What rhubarb, senna, or what purgative drug,
55 Would scour these English hence? Hear'st thou of them?

Seton   All that's been reported is confirmed.

Macbeth   I'll fight till the flesh is hacked from my bones! Give me my armor!

Seton   It isn't needed yet.

Macbeth   I'll put it on. Send out more scouts. Scour the country. Hang those who talk of fear. Give me my armor. [*To the* **Doctor**] How is your patient, doctor?

Doctor   Not so much sick, my lord, as troubled with numerous hallucinations that stop her from sleeping.

Macbeth   Cure her of that. Can't you remedy a diseased mind? Pull from the memory a sorrow that is rooted there? Rub out the troubles that are written on the brain? And with some sweet relaxing drug dispel what chokes the breast and weighs heavy on the heart?

Doctor   In these matters, the patient must take care of himself.

Macbeth   Throw medicine to the dogs! It's no use to me. [*To* **Seton**] Come, put my armor on. Give me my lance. Seton, find out more. Doctor, the thanes fly from me. [*To* **Seton** *again, impatiently*] Come on, sir; hurry up! [*Now to the* **Doctor**] If only, doctor, you could diagnose the sickness of my country! Purge it back to sound and pristine health! I would applaud you to the echo, and yet again. [*To* **Seton**] Pull it off, I tell you. [*To the* **Doctor**] Where's the rhubarb, senna or purgative drug that would flush out these English? Have you heard about them?

Doctor   Ay, my good lord; your royal preparation
Makes us hear something.

Macbeth   Bring it after me.
I will not be afraid of death and bane
Till Birnam forest come to Dunsinane.

[*Exeunt* **Macbeth** *and* **Seton**]

60 **Doctor**   Were I from Dunsinane away and clear,
Profit again should hardly draw me here.

[*Exit*]

Scene 4

Country near Birnam Wood. Drum and colours. Enter **Malcolm,
Siward, Macduff, Siward's son, Menteith, Caithness, Angus,
Lennox, Ross,** *and* **Soldiers,** *marching.*

Malcolm   Cousins, I hope, the days are near at hand
That chambers will be safe.

Menteith   We doubt it nothing.

Siward   What wood is this before us?

Menteith   The wood of Birnam.

Malcolm   Let every soldier hew him down a bough,
5   And bear't before him: thereby shall we shadow
The numbers of our host, and make discovery
Err in report of us.

Doctor Yes, my good lord. Your Majesty's preparations bring them to our notice.

Macbeth [*To* **Seton**, *impatiently refusing more armor*] Follow after me with it. I won't be afraid of death and disaster till Birnam Forest comes to Dunsinane!

Doctor [*To himself*] If I were clear away from Dunsinane, money wouldn't tempt me back again.

[*They go*]

Scene 4

The country near Birnam Wood, where the rebels have joined forces with Malcolm and Siward. **Malcolm, Siward, Macduff, Siward's son, Menteith, Caithness, Angus, Lennox, Ross** *and some* **Soldiers** *enter.*

Malcolm Kinsman, I hope the days are near at hand when we can sleep without fear of being murdered.

Menteith We have no doubt.

Siward What's this wood ahead of us?

Menteith Birnam Wood.

Malcolm Tell every soldier to cut down a bough for himself and to carry it in front. That will conceal the size of the army and make the scouts give false reports of us.

Soldier   It shall be done.

Siward   We learn no other but the confident tyrant
Keeps still in Dunsinane, and will endure
Our setting down before't.

10 **Malcolm**   'Tis his main hope:
For where there is advantage to be gone,
Both more and less have given him the revolt,
And none serve with him but constrained things
Whose hearts are absent too.

Macduff   Let our just censures
15 Attend the true event, and put we on
Industrious soldiership.

Siward   The time approaches,
That will with due decision make us know
What we shall say we have and what we owe.
Thoughts speculative their unsure hopes relate,
20 But certain issue strokes must arbitrate:
Towards which advance the war.

[Exeunt, marching]

Scene 5

Dunsinane. The court of the castle as before. Enter **Macbeth**,
Seton, *and* **Soldiers** *with drum and colours.*

Macbeth   Hang out our banners on the outward walls;
The cry is still 'They come'. our castle's strength
Will laugh a siege to scorn: here let them lie
Till famine and the ague eat them up:

Soldier   It shall be done.

Siward   All evidence suggests that the confident tyrant has settled in Dunsinane. He'll let us besiege it.

Malcolm   It's his only hope. Whenever they've had the chance to escape, men of all ranks have deserted him. Only mercenary wretches serve with him. Their hearts are elsewhere.

Macduff   Let us pass judgment after battle. Meanwhile, plan our strategy carefully.

Siward   We'll soon know how things really stand. Speculation is idle. Some issues can only be settled in battle. That being so – let's go to war!

[*They all march off*]

Scene 5

A court in Dunsinane Castle. **Macbeth, Seton** *and* **Soldiers** *enter.*

Macbeth   Hang out our banners on the outer walls. Still the cry is "Here they come!" Our castle is so strong that siege is laughable. Let them stay here till they're eaten with famine

5   Were they not forced with those that should be ours,
      We might have met them dareful, beard to beard,
      And beat them backward home.

                              [*A cry of women within*]

                                  What is that noise?

Seton   It is the cry of women, my good lord.

                                              [*Exit*]

Macbeth   I have almost forgot the taste of fears:
10   The time has been, my senses would have cooled
       To hear a night-shriek, and my fell of hair
       Would at a dismal treatise rouse and stir
       As life were in't: I have supped full with horrors;
       Direness, familiar to my slaughterous thoughts,
15   Cannot once start me.

       [*Re-enter* **Seton**]

                                  Wherefore was that cry?

Seton   The queen, my lord, is dead.

Macbeth   She should have died hereafter;
       There would have been a time for such a word.
       To-morrow, and to-morrow, and to-morrow,
20   Creeps in this petty pace from day to day,
       To the last syllable of recorded time;
       And all our yesterdays have lighted fools
       The way to dusty death. Out, out, brief candle!
       Life's but a walking shadow, a poor player
25   That struts and frets his hour upon the stage,
       And then is heard no more: it is a tale
       Told by an idiot, full of sound and fury,
       Signifying nothing.

and the plague! If they hadn't been reinforced by our deserters, we might have met them boldly, face-to-face, and sent them packing home. [*He hears a cry*] What's that noise?

Seton   It's the crying of women, my lord.

[*He leaves*]

Macbeth   I've almost forgotten the taste of fear. There was a time when shrieking in the night would have turned me cold. Groans would have raised my hair on end as if alive. I've had my fill of horrors. Ghastly sounds and sights are commonplace in my murderous thoughts. They can't shock me any more.

[**Seton** *returns*]

What was the reason for that cry?

Seton   The queen, my lord, is dead.

Macbeth   She would certainly have died sometime; some day that message would have come. Tomorrow . . . and tomorrow . . . and tomorrow . . . Life drags on from day to day to the end of time. All our yesterdays have merely lighted the way for fools to reach their graves. Out, out, brief candle. Life is but a walking shadow, a wretched actor who poses and rages for a short time on the stage and then is heard no more. It is a tale told by an idiot, full of sound and fury, signifying nothing.

[*Enter a* **Messenger**]

Thou com'st to use thy tongue; thy story quickly.

30 **Messenger**   Gracious my lord,
I should report that which I say I saw,
But know not how to do't.

Macbeth   Well, say, sir.

Messenger   As I did stand my watch upon the hill,
I looked toward Birnam, and anon, methought
35   The wood began to move.

Macbeth   Liar and slave!

Messenger   Let me endure your wrath, if't be not so:
Within this three mile may you see it coming.
I say, a moving grove.

Macbeth   If thou speak'st false,
Upon the next tree shalt thou hang alive,
40   Till famine cling thee: if thy speech be sooth,
I care not if thou dost for me as much.
I pull in resolution, and begin
To doubt th'equivocation of the fiend
That lies like truth: 'Fear not, till Birnam wood
45   Do come to Dunsinane'; and now a wood
Comes toward Dunsinane. Arm, arm, and out!
If this which he avouches does appear,
There is nor flying hence nor tarrying here.
I 'gin to be aweary of the sun,
50   And wish th'estate o'th' world were now undone.
Ring the alarum bell! Blow, wind! come, wrack!
At least we'll die with harness on our back.

[*Exeunt*]

[*A* **Messenger** *enters*]

You've come to use your tongue. Quick – your news.

Messenger   My gracious lord, I ought to report what I know that I saw, but I don't know how to do it.

Macbeth   Well, say it, sir!

Messenger   When I was on watch on the hill, I looked toward Birnam. Soon I thought the wood began to move.

Macbeth   Liar and slave!

Messenger   Let your anger come down on me if I'm wrong. You can see it coming not three miles away. I say it's a moving grove.

Macbeth   If you are lying, you'll hang alive on the next tree till you die of hunger! If what you say is true, I don't care if you do the same for me. I'm losing my confidence. I begin to doubt the deceptions of the devil, whose lies sound like truth. "Fear not till Birnam Wood comes to Dunsinane." And now a wood does come toward Dunsinane. To arms, to arms, and to the field! If what he says is true, there's no running away, nor hesitating here. The sun wearies me. The world can fall apart. Ring the alarm bell. Let the winds blow! Come, ruin! At least I'll die in armor!

[*They go*]

Scene 6

Dunsinane. Before the castle gate. Drum and colours. Enter
Malcolm, Siward, Macduff, *and their army, with boughs.*

Malcolm Now near enough: your leavy screens throw down,
   And show like those you are. You, worthy uncle,
   Shall with my cousin your right-noble son
   Lead our first battle: worthy Macduff and we
5 Shall take upon's what else remains to do,
   According to our order.

Siward   Fare you well.
   Do we but find the tyrant's power to-night,
   Let us be beaten, if we cannot fight.

Macduff Make all our trumpets speak; give them all breath,
10 Those clamorous harbingers of blood and death.

                               [*Exeunt*]

Scene 7

Another part of the field

Macbeth They have tied me to a stake; I cannot fly,
   But bear-like I must fight the course. What's he
   That was not born of woman? Such a one
   Am I to fear, or none.

   [*Enter* **Young Siward**]

5 **Young Siward** What is thy name?

Scene 6

Close to the walls of Dunsinane Castle. **Malcolm, Siward, Macduff** *and the army enter, carrying branches of trees.*

Malcolm Now we're near enough. Throw down your branches, and show yourselves as you are. [*To* **Siward**] You, worthy uncle, shall with my cousin, your truly noble son, lead the first encounter. Worthy Macduff and I will take charge of the rest, according to our plan.

Siward Farewell. If we find the tyrant's army before nightfall, may we be beaten if we're not prepared to fight!

Macduff Sound all our trumpets! Blow them all. Those clamorous heralds of blood and death!

[*They go*]

Scene 7

Another part of the field. **Macbeth** *enters.*

Macbeth They've tied me to a stake. I can't escape. Like a bear I must stand and fight. What kind of man is he who wasn't born of woman? That's the sort I'm to fear – or nobody.

[**Young Siward** *enters*]

Young Siward What is your name?

Macbeth   Thou'lt be afraid to hear it.

Young Siward   No; though thou call'st thyself a hotter name
   Than any is in hell.

Macbeth   My name's Macbeth.

Young Siward   The devil himself could not pronounce a title
   More hateful to mine ear.

Macbeth   No, nor more fearful;

10 **Young Siward**   Thou liest, abhorred tyrant; with my sword
   I'll prove the lie thou speak'st.

   [*They fight, and* **Young Siward** *is slain*]

Macbeth   Thou wast born of woman.
   But swords I smile at, weapons laugh to scorn,
   Brandished by man that's of a woman born.

   [*Alarums. Enter* **Macduff**]

Macduff   That way the noise is. Tyrant, show thy face!
15   If thou be'est slain and with no stroke of mine,
   My wife and children's ghosts will haunt me still.
   I cannot strike at wretched kerns, whose arms
   Are hired to bear their staves; either thou, Macbeth,
   Or else my sword with an unbattered edge
20   I sheathe again undeeded. There thou shouldst be;
   By this great clatter, one of greatest note
   Seems bruited. Let me find him, fortune!
   And more I beg not.

   [**Malcolm** *and* **Siward** *come up*]

Siward   This way, my lord; the castle's gently rendered:
25   The tyrant's people on both sides do fight,

Macbeth   You'll be afraid to hear it.

Young Siward   No – not even if the name you use is hotter than any known in hell.

Macbeth   My name's Macbeth.

Young Siward   The devil himself could not pronounce a name more hateful to my ear.

Macbeth   No, nor more frightening!

Young Siward   You're lying, you odious tyrant! I'll prove it's a lie with my sword!

[*They fight.* **Young Siward** *is killed*]

Macbeth   You were born of woman! I smile at swords and laugh scornfully at weapons when they are brandished by a man who's born of woman!

[*Sounds of war.* **Macduff** *enters, seeking out* **Macbeth**]

Macduff   The noise is that way – [*Shouting*] Tyrant, show your face! If you are killed and not by me, the ghosts of my wife and children will haunt me evermore! I can't fight with wretched mercenaries, who are hired to wield their clubs. Either it's you, Macbeth, or else I'll sheath my sword again, unused. [*Pointing*] You should be there, judging by the noise. It indicates a man of highest rank. Let me find him, fortune! I beg no more!

[*He goes. The sounds of war continue.* **Malcolm** *and* **Siward** *enter*]

Siward   This way, my lord. The castle has surrendered without a struggle. The tyrant's men fight on both sides. The noble

The noble thanes do bravely in the war,
The day almost itself professes yours,
And little is to do.

Malcolm   We have met with foes
That strike beside us.

Siward   Enter, sir, the castle.

[*Exeunt*]

[**Macbeth** *returns*]

30 **Macbeth**   Why should I play the Roman fool, and die
On mine own sword? whiles I see lives, the gashes
Do better upon them.

[*Enter* **Macduff**]

Macduff   Turn, hell-hound, turn.

Macbeth   Of all men else I have avoided thee:
But get thee back, my soul is too much charged
35 With blood of thine already.

Macduff   I have no words:
My voice is in my sword, thou bloodier villain
Than terms can give thee out!

[*They fight*]

Macbeth   Thou losest labour.
As easy mayst thou the intrenchant air
With thy keen sword impress as make me bleed:
40 Let fall thy blade on vulnerable crests,
I bear a charmed life, which must not yield
To one of woman born.

thanes fight bravely in the war. The day is almost yours. There's little else to do.

Malcolm   Some of the enemy have fought beside us.

Siward   Enter the castle, sir.

[*They go.* **Macbeth** *returns*]

Macbeth   Why should I act like a foolish Roman and die on my own sword? While I see living men, they suit my gashes better.

[**Macduff** *enters*]

Macduff   Turn, hellhound, turn!

Macbeth   Of all men, I've avoided you! Get back! There's too much blood of yours on my soul already!

Macduff   I have no words for you. My sword will speak for me, you bloodier villain than mere words can express!

[*They fight*]

Macbeth   You're wasting your energy! You could as easily wound the air with your sharp sword as make me bleed. Bring down your sword on vulnerable heads. I bear a charmed life, not to be surrendered to a man born of a woman!

Macduff   Despair thy charm,
And let the angel whom thou still hast served
Tell thee, Macduff was from his mother's womb
45   Untimely ripped.

Macbeth   Accursed be that tongue that tells me so,
For it hath cowed my better part of man!
And be these juggling fiends no more believed,
That palter with us in a double sense,
50   That keep the word of promise to our ear,
And break it to our hope. I'll not fight with thee.

Macduff   Then yield thee, coward,
And live to be the show and gaze o'th' time.
We'll have thee, as our rarer monsters are,
55   Painted upon a pole, and underwrit,
'Here may you see the tyrant'.

Macbeth   I will not yield,
To kiss the ground before young Malcolm's feet,
And to be baited with the rabble's curse.
Though Birnam wood be come to Dunsinane,
60   And thou opposed, being of no woman born,
Yet I will try the last. Before my body
I throw my warlike shield: lay on, Macduff,
And damned be him that first cries 'Hold, enough'.

[Exeunt, fighting]

Retreat and flourish. Enter, with drum and colours, **Malcolm,
Siward, Ross, Thanes** *and* **Soldiers**.

Malcolm   I would the friends we miss were safe arrived.

65 **Siward**   Some must go off: and yet, by these I see,
So great a day as this is cheaply bought.

Malcolm   Macduff is missing, and your noble son.

Macduff   Lose hope in your charm! And let the devil you serve tell you this: Macduff was taken from his mother's womb before her time!

Macbeth   Damnation to the tongue that tells me that! It has daunted my manly courage. These devils who juggle with words: they lie. They trifle with us in a double sense. They sustain us with promises, then dash our hopes.

Macduff   Then surrender, coward! And live to be an exhibition, a sideshow freak! We'll have your picture up on a pole like one of our rarer monsters, and written underneath will be, "Here you can see the tyrant!"

Macbeth   I won't surrender, to kiss the ground beneath young Malcolm's feet and to be taunted by the curses of the rabble. Even if Birnam Wood has come to Dunsinane, and you are my opponent – not born of woman – I'll keep fighting to the end. I throw my warlike shield before my body. Fight on, Macduff, and damned be the one who first cries, "Stop, enough!"

[*They go off, fighting*]

[**Malcolm, Siward, Ross, Thanes** *and* **Soldiers** *enter*]

Malcolm   I wish our missing friends were safely here.

Siward   Some must die. But from these I see, a day as great as this is cheaply bought.

Malcolm   Macduff is missing – and your noble son.

Ross   Your son, my lord, has paid a soldier's debt:
He only lived but till he was a man,
70   The which no sooner had his prowess confirmed
In the unshrinking station where he fought,
But like a man he died.

Siward   Then he is dead?

Ross   Ay, and brought off the field: your cause of sorrow
Must not be measured by his worth, for then
75   It hath no end.

Siward   Had he his hurts before?

Ross   Ay, on the front.

Siward   Why then, God's soldier be he!
Had I as many sons as I have hairs,
I would not wish them to a fairer death:
And so his knell is knolled.

Malcolm   He's worth more sorrow,
80   And that I'll spend for him.

Siward   He's worth no more.
They say he parted well and paid his score:
And so God be with him! Here comes newer comfort.

[*Re-enter* **Macduff**, *with* **Macbeth**'*s head*]

Macduff   Hail, king! for so thou art. Behold where stands
Th'usurper's cursed head: the time is free:
85   I see thee compassed with thy kingdom's pearl,
That speak my salutation in their minds;
Whose voice I desire aloud with mine:
Hail, king of Scotland!

All   Hail, king of Scotland!

Ross   Your son, my lord, has died like a soldier. He only lived to reach his manhood. He'd no sooner proved his valor in the battle station, where he fought unyieldingly, than like a man he died.

Siward   Then he is dead?

Ross   Yes, and brought off the field. Don't measure your sorrow by his worth, for then your grief would be infinite.

Siward   Were his wounds in front?

Ross   Yes, in front.

Siward   Well, then, let him be a soldier of God. If I had as many sons as I've got hairs, I wouldn't wish a fairer death for them. His bell is tolled.

Malcolm   He's worth more sorrow, and I'll give it him!

Siward   He's worth no more. They say he died well and paid his score. And so God be with him. Here comes newer comfort.

[**Macduff** *enters, with* **Macbeth**'*s head on a pole*]

Macduff   [*To* **Malcolm**] Hail, King! For such you are. See where the usurper's cursed head stands! The world can breathe again. [*Looking at the thanes*] I see you surrounded by your country's pearls. They speak my greeting in their minds. I call upon them to join aloud with me: "Hail, King of Scotland!"

Thanes   Hail, King of Scotland!

[*Trumpets sound*]

Malcolm   We shall not spend a large expense of time
90   Before we reckon with your several loves,
        And make us even with you. My thanes and kinsmen,
        Henceforth be earls, the first that ever Scotland
        In such an honour named. What's more to do,
        Which would be planted newly with the time,
95   As calling home our exiled friends abroad
        That fled the snares of watchful tyranny,
        Producing forth the cruel ministers
        Of this dead butcher and his fiend-like queen,
        Who, as 'tis thought, by self and violent hands
100   Took off her life; this, and what needful else
        That calls upon us, by the grace of Grace
        We will perform in measure, time, and place:
        So thanks to all at once, and to each one,
        Whom we invite to see us crowned at Scone.

                                        [*Exeunt*]

Malcolm   We shall not keep you waiting long before we
express our gratitude to you all, individually, and settle our
accounts. My thanes and kinsmen, henceforth you shall be
earls, the first that Scotland ever named. The other things we
have to do in these new circumstances – such as calling home
our exiled friends, who fled the country, and seeking out the
cruel agents of this dead butcher and his fiendish queen, who
took her own life, so they say this and whatever else we will
perform at the appropriate time and place. So thanks to you all
– collectively and individually. We invite you to see us
crowned at Scone.

[*They go*]

Activities

Characters

Search the text to find answers to the following questions. They will help you to form personal opinions about the major characters in the play. *Record any relevant quotations in Shakespeare's own words, making sure you divide the lines in the right places.*

Macbeth

1 a Who first refers to Macbeth by name?
   b Do you think this has any significance?

2 What words are first used to describe Macbeth as a soldier?

3 Find other speeches or episodes in the play that illustrate Macbeth's bravery and courage.

4 a Is Macbeth ever afraid?
   b If so, find examples of the kind of thing that frightens him.

5 Find an occasion when Macbeth's manly courage is used by another to influence his behavior.

6 How does Macbeth react when the Third Witch speaks of him as "king hereafter!"? Give an explanation for his response.

7 Immediately after he learns he is Thane of Cawdor (the second prophecy),
   a what thoughts about the third prophecy go through Macbeth's mind?
   b what hints are there in his speeches about his intended actions in the future?

8 Consider what Duncan says at the end of Act I Scene 4. Compare this with Macbeth's reputation as described by others.

9 Lady Macbeth knows her husband very well and analyzes his character in Act I Scene 5. List the points she makes about him.

10 Macbeth fights bravely, but when he thinks, he can be indecisive.
a List his changes of mind about Duncan's murder.
b Find the speech in which he decides to be resolute in action in the future.

11 Read Macbeth's soliloquy (words spoken to himself) at the beginning of Act I Scene 7.
a What does it tell us of his moral scruples?
b What are his reasons for not proceeding with his murderous plans?
c What, according to Macbeth, is his motive for the proposed assassination?

12 Macbeth has a number of hallucinations in the play. What does each tell us about the state of his mind at the time?

13 Consider Macbeth's relationship with his wife
a before the murder
b immediately after it
c during the banquet scene
d thereafter.

14 At what point in the play does Macbeth resolve to act without reference to his wife's advice? What kind of suffering does he think he will spare Lady Macbeth by keeping her in ignorance?

15 The guests at the banquet scene seem to accept Lady Macbeth's explanation for Macbeth's strange behavior. From what Macbeth says in his fits, what might an astute listener deduce?

16 What causes Macbeth to decide to override his conscience? Who suffers as a consequence?

17 Does Macbeth suffer any regret – or any remorse – toward the end of the play?

18 In what respects does blind anger manifest itself as Macbeth approaches his end?

19 During his lifetime, what price did Macbeth pay for his ambition?

20 Does it do full justice to Macbeth to describe him simply as a "dead butcher"? Can anything be said to attract our sympathy or pity?

Lady Macbeth

1 What examples are there in the text of the affectionate relationship between Lady Macbeth and her husband?

2 What speeches and lines suggest that Lady Macbeth is a capable planner and organizer?

3 What womanly/feminine traits can you detect in
a her behavior
b what she says

4 What examples of Lady Macbeth's skills as a hostess are to be found in the play?

5 How does Lady Macbeth contrive to change Macbeth's "We will proceed no further in this business" to "I am settled, and bend up each corporal agent to this terrible feat"? (Act I Scene 7)

6 a Do the first lines of Act II Scene 2 have any bearing on Lady Macbeth's ability to sustain Macbeth immediately after Duncan's murder?
b Is there any evidence in the scene to suggest that her iron will is suppressing other and more natural instincts?

7 Supposing Lady Macbeth's fainting fit in Act II Scene 3 is a pretense, what is skillful about her timing?

8 a In what scene does Lady Macbeth begin to show signs of realizing that crime does not pay?
   b In the same scene, what line suggests that her powers are diminishing?

9 If Macbeth is strong in action, Lady Macbeth is strong in mind. Illustrate this from her behavior in the banquet scene.

10 What connection is there between the last words she speaks in Act III Scene 4 and her behavior as reported in Act V Scene 1?

11 Each of Lady Macbeth's sleepwalking speeches has echoes of former words and deeds.
    a Trace them all back to their sources.
    b Do you think they confirm that she was a "fiend-like queen"?

12 a A line in Act II Scene 2 indicates that Lady Macbeth foresaw her fate. What is it?
    b The Doctor in Act V Scene 1 also hints correctly at her future fate: trace the line and relate it to the manner of her death.

Banquo

1 Read carefully the references to Banquo in the early scenes of the play, and consider the way he speaks and behaves when in Macbeth's company.
   a What do the two men have in common?
   b In what ways are they different?

2 Examine in detail the reactions of Banquo during the encounter with the Weird Sisters in Act I Scene 3. Macbeth ought to have heeded some of Banquo's wise words: what were they?

3   How can we tell from his speeches in Act II Scene 1 that Banquo has been disturbed by the prophecies? How does his response differ from Macbeth's?

4   In which speech does Banquo first express his suspicions about Macbeth? Is there any suggestion that he, too, could fall victim to the Witches' temptations?

5   Trace all Macbeth's references to Banquo's positive qualities. Are they accurate observations?

6   List the reasons why Macbeth fears Banquo and why he believes he must kill him.

7   In Act II Scene 3, Banquo resolved to "question this most bloody piece of work, / To know it further." If he had suspected Macbeth, what evidence would he have submitted to an inquiry?

8   The real Banquo was said to be an ancestor of James I, so the king would not expect Shakespeare to present him unfavorably. Trace all Banquo's characteristics that would please the monarch.

9   Banquo is dramatically significant in both life and death. Identify points in the text where this is evident.

10   Some critics think Banquo could have done more to restrain Macbeth. Identify episodes in the play where Banquo might have been more influential.

Duncan

1   The Duncan in Holinshed's *Chronicles* was a young, weak man. What lines in the play indicate that the Duncan of *Macbeth* was a character of Shakespeare's own creation?

2   Take each speech of Duncan's in Act I Scene 4 and say what it reveals about his character.

3   After his death, reference is made to "the gracious Duncan." Examine Act I Scene 6 and list examples of this gentle quality.

4 Duncan is generous, with both praise and gifts. Find examples of both from the text.

5 What does Duncan tell us of the duties and privileges of kingship?

Macduff

1 Is there any one line in Act II Scene 3 that could be said to be the starting point of Macduff's opposition to Macbeth?

2 From the evidence in Act II Scene 4, show how cautiously Macduff revealed his suspicions.

3 What were the reasons for Macbeth's distrust of Macduff? Find the lines which

   a show Macduff did not cooperate with the new king as Banquo did, and

   b most forthrightly indicate his shrewd understanding of Macbeth's ruthlessness.

4 Consider the discussion in Act IV Scene 2 about Macduff's flight to England. Is there an answer to Malcolm's question in the next scene, "Why in that rawness left you wife and child"?

5 Show from his speeches in Act IV Scene 3 that Macduff is a dedicated patriot.

Malcolm

1 The first two speeches of Act IV Scene 3 seem to indicate a character contrast. In the light of events, is what Malcolm says a true indicator of his character?

2 List the qualities which Malcolm says he possesses which would make him unfit to be king.

3 List the qualities which Malcolm later claims to be his.

4 Quote some instances of Malcolm as a positive thinker, possessed of powers of leadership.

Themes and images

In addition to creating characters and plots, playwrights often use figurative language to give feeling and atmosphere to a play. When an idea is repeated, it can build up into a theme which gives us a new viewpoint on the play as a whole.

Darkness

In *Macbeth* Shakespeare often refers to darkness, both real and imagined:

1 "Come, thick night,
   And pall thee in the dunnest smoke of hell,"

   Act I Scene 5 lines 49–50

2 "That darkness does the face of earth entomb,
   When living light should kiss it?"

   Act II Scene 4 lines 9–10

3 "Stars, hide your fires!
   Let not light see my black and deep desires;"

   Act I Scene 4 lines 50–51

a Which feelings and thoughts associated with darkness do you think Shakespeare is calling up in each of these three examples?

b Find as many more references as you can to darkness and light.

c What atmosphere is Shakespeare building up in the play with these references?

The unnatural

1 "And make my seated heart knock at my ribs,
   Against the use of nature?"

   Act I Scene 3 lines 136–37

2 " 'Tis unnatural,
Even like the deed that's done."

Act II Scene 4 lines 10–11

3 " 'Gainst nature still!"

Act II Scene 4 line 27

a What are the emotions that the speakers in these examples feel when an act is against nature?

b Find as many other references as you can to this theme.

c What do you think is the response Shakespeare is seeking in these references to order and disorder?

Blood

Blood makes us think of death and violence.

a How many references to blood can you find in the play?
b How do they establish the play's atmosphere?

Animals and birds

Shakespeare refers to a number of animals, reptiles and birds, some of which are heard and seen in the play, some of which are used for comparison.

1 "The raven himself is hoarse
That croaks the fatal entrance of Duncan"

Act I Scene 5 lines 37–38

2 "look like the innocent flower,
But be the serpent under't."

Act I Scene 5 lines 64–65

3 "It was the owl that shrieked, the fatal bellman,"

Act II Scene 2 line 3

a What do the creatures in these examples have in common?
b Find as many other similar references as you can.
c What do you conclude about Shakespeare's use of animal, bird and reptile imagery?

213

Clothing

Clothes can make us look different and feel different; they can express what we feel or hide what we feel. They can be comfortable or uncomfortable; they can fit well or badly. In *Macbeth*, Shakespeare often uses clothes in similes or metaphors.

1 "The thane of Cawdor lives: why do you dress me
   In borrowed robes?"

Act I Scene 3 lines 108–9

2 "New honours come upon him,
   Like our strange garments, cleave not to their mould
   But with the aid of use."

Act I Scene 3 lines 144–46

In 1, Macbeth is using the way we feel in borrowed clothes to express his discomfort at being called by someone else's title. In 2, Banquo is using the feeling of wearing new clothes to help us imagine more clearly how Macbeth feels about the new honors which he needs time to get used to.

a Find other examples of clothes used for simile or metaphor.
b Choose four of them and explain how the clothing image in each one makes the speaker's meaning more vivid.
c What do you think is the overall effect of this repeated use of clothes as an image?

Disease and sickness

Another recurrent theme in *Macbeth* is illness.

1 "If thou couldst, Doctor, cast
   The water of my land, find her disease,
   And purge it to a sound and pristine health,"

Act V Scene 3 lines 50–52

2 "What rhubarb, senna, or what purgative drug,
   Would scour these English hence?"

Act V Scene 3 lines 54–55

a In these examples, who or what is said to be ill?
b Find as many other references to sickness or disease as you can.
c Why do you think Shakespeare referred to illness so often in this play?

Weather

Elizabethan theatergoers saw their plays on fine days and, at Shakespeare's Globe Theatre, in the open air. When he wanted to create a sense of a different sort of weather, he had to do it in the language the actors spoke:

1 "When shall we three meet again
   In thunder, lightning, or in rain?"

Act I Scene 1 lines 1–2

2 "So foul and fair a day I have not seen."

Act I Scene 3 line 38

a Find as many examples as you can of the weather the characters talk about.
b How do references to the weather contribute to the effectiveness of the play?
c What sort of weather is referred to most often, and why?

Close reading

Read the original Shakespeare and (if necessary) the modern transcription to gain an understanding of the speeches and extracts below. Then concentrate entirely on the original in answering the questions.

1 *If it were done, when 'tis done,* (*Act I Scene 7 lines 1–28*)

   a Why do you think the first words of this speech are mostly monosyllables?

   b To "trammel up" is to trap in a net. How does the verb initiate a series of images that help us to understand Macbeth's distinction between this life and the next?

   c "Shoal" is sometimes printed as "school," which originally had the same meaning. Which do you prefer? Would you be influenced in your choice by the references to teaching in the lines that follow?

   d Where has Shakespeare used personification? What effect does this have?

   e What similes has Shakespeare used? How have they added to his meaning?

   f After the word "babe," there is a comma. Shakespeare's punctuation is sometimes more related to recommended pauses in the actor's delivery than the textual meaning. Do you approve of the comma here?

   g Discuss the effect of the biblical references.

   h Discuss the effect of the references to weather.

   i Discuss the effect of the horsemanship metaphor.

2 *Is this a dagger which I see before me,* (*Act II Scene 1 lines 33–64*)

   a Sight and touch are key senses in this soliloquy. Note the number of times Shakespeare refers to them.

b At what point does Macbeth finally realize that he is dealing with "a dagger of the mind"?

c In Elizabethan times, beds were four-posters with curtains. Does this fully explain the reference to "curtain'd sleep," or could there be another interpretation?

d There are several military images in the speech. Identify them. What effect do they have?

e Shakespeare occasionally uses rhyme to indicate the end of a scene, to make certain lines of great significance stand out from the text, and to relieve tension. Comment on the use of rhyme in this soliloquy in the light of this information.

f If this soliloquy were to be divided under two headings, one "hallucination" and the other "resolution," where would the division be?

g In Shakespeare's day, *Macbeth* would have been performed in broad daylight. Which lines would help the audience to imagine the nocturnal setting?

h The bell rings offstage. From the evidence in the scenes immediately before and immediately after this one, imagine what has led up to this signal.

3 *To be thus is nothing, | But to be safely thus:* (*Act III Scene 1 lines 47–71*)

a Explain why "safely" in the first line has a special emphasis.

b Is there a line which suggests that Macbeth believes Banquo is plotting against him?

c Which line reveals Macbeth's belief that he may lose the throne through violence?

d Which line refers to his uneasy conscience?

e Which lines reveal that he knows the enormity of his crime?

4 *She should have died hereafter;* (*Act V Scene 5 lines 17–28*)

a Most editors think the first line means "She had to die sometime." Others, taking into account the second line, think it could mean "She died at an inappropriate time – she should have died later, when it was more convenient." Discuss the alternative meanings.

b "Such a word": as what?

c What is gained by repeating "tomorrow" three times?

d In the next line, how does Shakespeare sustain what he has been at pains to gain?

e The meaning of "brief candle" is contained in the previous line. What is it?

f One editor thinks "dusty" death should be "dusky" death. What would be gained, and what lost, by adopting this emendation?

g Explain "Life's but a walking shadow." Can you explain why this image follows from the previous lines?

h In what sense is the player a "poor" player? Why is he said to "strut" and "fret"?

i "Life" says Macbeth, "is meaningless." Why is Shakespeare's way of saying this so powerful?

5 (*Act I Scene 7 line 59*)

Macbeth: *If we should fail?*
Lady M: *We fail?*

This is the punctuation according to the Folio Edition of 1623. Some actresses drop the second question mark in favor of a full stop. How does this change the meaning? Which do you prefer?

6 (*Act II Scene 2 line 14*)

Macbeth: *I have done the deed. Didst thou not hear a noise?*

a Consider the employment of silence and simple exclamation to create an atmosphere of tension and fear.

   b   Contrast this staccato dialog with Macbeth's subsequent speeches, ending "Macbeth shall sleep no more." How does Shakespeare convey Macbeth's mounting terror?

7 *(Act II Scene 2 lines 61–63)*

Macbeth: *No; this my hand will rather*
                The multitudinous seas incarnadine,
                Making the green one red.

   a   Discuss the use of the multisyllabic words, and contrast them with the short ones. What is achieved?

   b   In the Folio Edition, there is a comma after "one." Most editions put it after "green." Some leave it out altogether. Discuss the various interpretations.

8 *The Porter's Speech*   *(Act II Scene 3 lines 1–18)*

   a   The intrusion of bawdy comedy is at the very point when the audience is steeped in horror. Why do you think Shakespeare did this?

   b   The knocking. Explain why this has been highly regarded for its dramatic significance.

   c   "If a man were porter of hell-gate . . ." Comment.

9 *We have scotched the snake, not killed it:* *(Act III Scene 2 lines 13–26)*

Closely examine this speech as Shakespeare wrote it, and compare it with the modern translation. What is lost in turning dramatic poetry into prose?

10 Similarly, compare the two versions of the "Come, seeling night" speech later in the same scene (lines 46–56).

11 Choose some speeches in the banquet scene (Act III Scene 4) that bring out the aptness of Shakespeare's expressions.

12 Act V Scene 1 is mostly in prose. What is gained (or lost) by this?

Examination questions

1   "Things bad begun make strong themselves by ill."
    Although Macbeth gives this assurance to his wife, is it true
    in his own case?

2   What prevents *Macbeth* from being nothing more than the
    story of a ruthless and ambitious murderer?

3   Give an account of Lady Macbeth's words and actions in
    Act I Scenes 5, 6 and 7. Stress the qualities in her character
    that may be said to have influenced Macbeth.

4   Choose one scene from *Macbeth* which you regard as out-
    standing for its tension and its atmosphere. Show how
    these qualities are achieved.

5   Describe the scene in which the Apparitions appear, and
    explain its dramatic effectiveness.

6   Summarize Macbeth's words and actions after the death of
    Lady Macbeth, paying particular attention to his changing
    state of mind.

7   "A gloomy play, full of darkness and evil." How far do you
    agree with this comment on *Macbeth*?

8   Give an account of Act I Scene 2 and say what you learn
    from it of Macbeth's character and reputation.

9   Refer in detail to three occasions when Macbeth is affected
    by his imagination.

10 What do you see as the most significant features of the first
    two scenes of Act II?

11 "The red of blood, and the black of darkness" have been
    identified as theme colors of the play. How far would you
    agree?

12 Macbeth in defeat is described as "this dead butcher." What case could be made out for excusing or pitying him?

13 Of what importance to the play are Banquo and Macduff? Show how they differ in character.

14 Describe the scene in which Lady Macduff and her family are murdered. How has Shakespeare made it tense and moving?

15 Referring as closely as you can to the text, show what Macbeth reveals of his character and motives in his soliloquies.

16 The atmosphere of Macbeth is created partly by repeated references to blood and darkness. Which of these have struck you most forcibly?

17 How is the theme of the breakdown of the natural order of things brought out and sustained in *Macbeth*?

18 For perhaps two-thirds of the play, Lady Macbeth, the "fiend-like queen," appalls us. After the sleepwalking scene we may be inclined to pity her. Do you agree or disagree? Make out a full case for your point of view.

19 Lady Macbeth is confident of her own ability to conquer natural instincts, and of her capacity to manipulate her husband, at the start of the play. Show how, by the end of it, she is shown to be doubly mistaken.

20 Many passages in *Macbeth* have been admired for their powerful language. Choose two which have impressed you, and explain in detail how they have enhanced your appreciation of Shakespeare's ability to create character and/or establish atmosphere.

One-word-answer quiz

1 Who was called "Bellona's bridegroom"?

2 What, according to Hecate, is "a mortal's chiefest enemy"?

3 What was the name of the King of Norway?

4 What did the sailor's wife munch?

5 What was the name of Macbeth's father?

6 Of what county was Malcolm made prince?

7 Where was the castle to which Duncan went after the victory?

8 To which country did Donalbain flee?

9 What was the word that Macbeth told Lady Macbeth he could not utter?

10 Where was Macbeth crowned?

11 Did Macduff attend the coronation?

12 Who or what was "the fatal bellman"?

13 At which entrance to Macbeth's castle did Macduff and Lennox knock?

14 Who was first to see the murdered Duncan after Macbeth and his wife?

15 Over how many years did the memory of the Old Man stretch?

16 How many men attacked and killed Banquo?

17 How many nights did the Doctor have to wait in order to see Lady Macbeth sleepwalking?

18 What is "a tale told by an idiot, full of sound and fury, signifying nothing"?

19 On the night of Duncan's murder, who lay in "the second chamber"?

20 Where was Macduff's castle?

21 What present did Duncan give to Lady Macbeth?

22 According to Lady Macbeth, whom did Duncan resemble as he slept?

What's missing?

Complete the following quotations:

1 Come what come may . . .
2 Thrice to thine, and thrice to mine,
   And thrice again, to . . .
3 There's husbandry in heaven . . .
4 What thou wouldst highly, That wouldst thou . . .
5 Go bid thy mistress, when my drink is ready, She . . .
6 Words to the heat of deeds . . .
7 The Thane of Cawdor lives: why . . .?
8 What he hath lost . . . hath won.
9 This supernatural soliciting . . .
10 Fair is foul, and . . .
11 Hear it not, Duncan, for it is a knell . . .
12 Lesser than Macbeth and . . .
13 Let's briefly put on manly readiness, And . . .
14 Yet who would have thought the old man . . .?
15 Duncan is in his grave. After life's . . . he sleeps well.
16 All our yesterdays have . . .
17 We'll have thee as our rarer monsters are, / Painted upon a
   pole, and underwrit " . . ."
18 Lay on, Macduff . . .
19 Still it cried " . . ." to all the house.
20 All the perfumes of Arabia . . .
21 A little . . . clears us of this deed
22 Nought's had, all's spent, / Where our desire . . .
23 Now does he feel his title / Hang loose about him, like . . .
24 Double, double toil and trouble; . . .